KT-499-651

CONTENTS

—'The African storyteller may employ . . . the accompaniment of mime or graphic language, or even music.'

General Introduction

In this book Africa is taken as that part south of the Sahara otherwise known as Negro Africa. This excludes the Berberized areas to the north, also Egypt and Ethiopia.

Story-telling is found everywhere, while art occurs mainly in West Africa and the Congo area, where the people lead a more settled, agricultural life, favourable to the accumulation of possessions, including carvings. In East and South Africa a more nomadic, pastoral way of life prevails, with a consequent economy of chattels. Yet South Africa is still the chief area for rock paintings even though increasing numbers are being found elsewhere.

Some general remarks apply to the whole of Negro Africa. Africa is moving into the mid-twentieth century at a headlong pace, attempting to cram into eighty-odd years the assimilation of a Western European-type civilization that took Europe five to eight hundred years to develop. So when I describe conditions in any area, I am usually describing the 'ethnographical present' – that is to say, the conditions obtaining before the European way of life prevailed.

It was in this context that the tales evolved, and were collected by missionaries and anthropologists. The old tribal religions, rules and customs formed the background for the people that told these tales, before Islam or Christianity or European materialism destroyed that framework.

The African way of life is largely agricultural and pastoral, with emphasis on one or the other as local conditions and cultures dictate. Hunting and fishing are also practised, though the Pygmies of the Congo and the Bushmen of the Kalahari are almost the only remaining African peoples to live by hunting and gathering alone. Agriculture is mainly the women's concern; in a pastoral society the men normally tend the herds. Men also hunt and fish and do any fighting that is necessary. Children start helping at an early age by herding animals, scaring birds from crops, and other light duties. Initiation ceremonies, to mark the transition from childhood to adult life, are widespread.

Stories are commonly told in the evening when the day's work is done. The following tales suffer from being in print inasmuch as they lack the accompaniment of mime, graphic language or even music that the African storyteller uses.

There is little evidence that storytellers are a privileged class, but there are two main kinds. The first would be a priest or elder who knew the oral traditions, history and literature of the tribe, and who might tell stories of tribal origins or to account for their customs. In some cases these oral traditions of tribal or dynastic history go back 500 years or more and may have a genuine foundation in fact.

The other type, the storyteller proper, might be a professional in the more Arabized parts of Africa. He would tell chiefly the trickster or culture-hero type of tale or a cosmological myth. African myths are realistic and down-to-earth: indeed, the gods themselves live on earth.

Tales are not used as a vehicle to express wish-fulfilment, the unfairness of life is accepted, the hero will not necessarily triumph, and wrongs may go unchecked. This last is true of the popular trickster type of story. Kwaku Ananse of Ghana, who was at the same time a man and a spider, is well known; the same adventures recur all over the continent with Tortoise and Hare (alias Brer Rabbit) as protagonists.

The bow, quiverful of arrows, bag, and digging-stick are the basic tools of the Bushmen in the Kalahari Desert.

Bushman and Hottentot tribes

The Bushmen are the oldest surviving African race. Now they are restricted to the Kalahari desert and the adjacent parts of Angola and South-West Africa, where they retreated before the Bantu (eleventh century onwards) and Dutch settlers (seventeenth century onwards). As many as 50,000 are now thought to survive there, mostly keeping to the original way of life, despite the influence of Bantu culture.

Their appearance is very distinctive. They are short, the men averaging sixty-two inches in height, their skin is yellowish-brown, and wrinkles very easily, their hair grows in tight tufts or 'peppercorns', exposing the scalp between. Lumbar lordosis causes prominent buttocks and in the women favours the development of steatopygia – accumulated fat on buttocks and thighs while the rest of the body may be thin.

Bushmen live in wandering bands of up to fifty persons, led by the older and more experienced men. As they live purely by hunting and gathering, their life is nomadic, but each band keeps to its own territory and waterholes. In hunting, the men's chief weapon is the bow; the arrows are tipped with poison made from the grub or chrysalis of a certain beetle. Throwing-sticks and spears, snares, traps and pitfalls are also used. The women gather vegetables such as the *tsamma* melon, also lizards and grubs, using a pointed digging stick, sometimes weighted with a perforated stone. Fire is made with fire-sticks. Food is shared by all the band, though the man who kills an animal may claim the skin for clothing. This is just a covering for the pudenda and a cloak for both sexes. Ostrich egg-shells are used to make beads, or as water-bottles to carry when on trek or to bury as reserves.

Little is known of Bushman religion – they pray to the Moon, etc., and have mythical beings, chiefly Mantis, who is a sort of culture-hero and personification of natural forces, especially rain-making. They have rituals for rain or hunting.

Bushmen love dancing, which they accompany with singing and clapping; also music, mainly from the musical bow. They are excellent mimics, whether in hunting, with the help of an animal skin, to stalk their quarry, or in dancing.

The language of Bushmen and Hottentots is characterized by a number of different 'clicks'.

Bushman paintings, which were still being painted about 100 years ago are often of high artistic merit. Many show

Bushman painting showing two Bushmen wearing the heads and skins of antelopes, for either hunting or ritual purposes.

cattle-raids, dances, and mythical beasts but mostly they depict the animals the Bushmen hunted. Usually the paintings are very small, averaging three to six inches. As they are mostly on cliff overhangs, it is likely that few are of great antiquity.

The Hottentots used to be thought a different race, but now 'Hottentot' seems to be considered a cultural and linguistic term. The main cultural difference is that they are pastoral, keeping herds of cattle and fat-tailed sheep. The need for fresh pastures entails some nomadism, but they lead a more settled life than the Bushmen. Their material culture is more advanced: they smelt and work iron, make wooden pots and vessels, and weave baskets and mats to cover their huts.

The origin of death
(Hottentot, South Africa).
They say that once upon a time, the Moon sent an insect to men, saying, 'Go to men and tell them, "As I die and dying live, so you shall also die and dying live!"'

The insect started off with the message, but as it was

Decorated water-vessel and string of beads made of ostrich egg-shells, also the only known Bushman painting on bone.

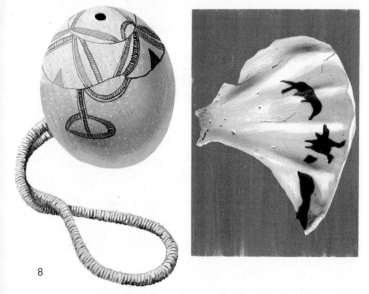

Rock painting of a Bushman hunting scene, with an antelope caught in a net.

going on its way it was overtaken by the hare who asked, 'Where are you going?'

The insect answered, 'The Moon has sent me as a messenger to men, to tell them that as she dies and dying lives, so shall they also die and dying live.'

The hare said, 'As you are slow and an awkward runner, let me go.' With these words he ran off, and when he came to the place where men lived, he said, 'I am sent by the Moon to tell you, "As I die and wholly perish, in the same way you also shall die and come to an end."'

The hare then returned to the Moon and told her what he had said to men. The Moon scolded him, saying, 'Do you dare to tell the people a thing which I have not said?'

With these words the Moon picked up a piece of wood and struck the hare on the nose. Since that day the hare's nose has been split, but men still believe what he told them.

9

How Elephant married a Nama woman, who deceived him

(Hottentot, South Africa)

It is said that Elephant fell in love with a Nama woman and married her. Her two brothers came to visit her secretly, but, fearing for their safety, she hid them in the firewood.

Then she said, 'Since I have married into this family, I beg of you, has the ram, the one-without-hair-at-the-knees, been killed for me?' The blind mother-in-law answered her, 'She speaks now of things that were not spoken of and I smell the smell of a Nama.' So the woman answered her mother-in-law, 'Should I not anoint myself in the old way and sprinkle myself with incense?' And the mother-in-law answered, 'Hum, my son's sweetheart says things that she used not to say.'

Just then, Elephant, who had been in the field, came home and behaved as if he had found out that the woman's two brothers had come. He rubbed himself against the house. Then the wife said, 'What I did not do of old, I do now. Which day did you kill the ram for me, and when did I anoint myself and sprinkle myself with my incense?' Thereupon the mother-in-law said to him, 'Things which used not to be spoken about are spoken now; therefore give her what she asks for.'

So the ram was killed. And the woman herself grilled it.

That night she asked her mother-in-law, 'How do you breathe when you sleep the sleep of life, and how do you breathe when you sleep the sleep of death?' And the mother-in-law said, 'Hum, this is an evening rich in conversation. When we sleep the sleep of death we breathe *sui sui,* and when we sleep the sleep of life we breathe *choo awaba, choo awaba.'*

Then the woman prepared all her things while the others were sleeping. When they snored heavily in the *sui sui* sleep, she got up and said to her brothers, 'The people are sleeping the sleep of death, let us make ready!' So the two brothers got up and went out, and all the packing was done in silence. Then, with the two brothers, who stood ready to go, she went among the flock, dividing it, and leaving the Elephant, her husband, only a cow, a sheep and a goat. Then she said to the cow, 'Do not cry as though you were only one, if you

A Bushman painting showing elephants, tsessebe antelopes and humans. The central elephant is about six inches long.

do not desire my death.' She said the same to the sheep and the goat. Then the woman and her brothers moved on with all the flock. Now, the animals that had been left behind cried and cried noisily in the night, and made as much noise as if they were all there, and Elephant thought all of them really were there. When he got up at daybreak, he saw that his wife had gone off with everything, so he grabbed a stick and said to his mother, 'If I fall, the earth will resound with a thud.' And he pursued them.

When his wife and her brothers saw him coming close, they turned aside, but found a great rock which barred the way. Thereupon the woman said, 'We are people behind whom a big company of travellers is following, so Rock of my forefathers, spread out to both sides for us!' The rock parted, and then when all had gone through, it closed again.

Elephant soon reached the rock and said, 'Rock of my forefathers, open for me too!' The rock opened and when he had entered, closed again. There Elephant died. The earth resounded with a thud. His mother at home said, 'It has happened as my oldest son foretold. The earth has just resounded with a thud.'

This Bushman painting of elands shows their mastery of shading and form. Superimposed elands were probably painted later.

This terra-cotta head from Nok, bronze torso from Ife, and bronze head from Benin are early masterpieces of African art.

West Africa

West Africa extends from the southern fringe of the Sahara to the sea, and from Senegal in the west to the Cameroon border in the east.

Politically, this is a confused part of Africa, and tribal boundaries do not coincide with political ones. In the northern part of the area, where the Islamic empires of the Middle Ages have left an aftermath of Moslem influence and Emirate rule, the Sudanese Negro population may be mixed to some

There is acute observation of life in these fine wooden palace doors, ten feet high, from the Yoruba of Nigeria.

extent with Hamitic stock (Berber, Tuareg or Fulani). Conditions there are very different from those on the coast and its immediate hinterland, where there is tropical forest rather than savannah turning to scrub and desert. This area is in effect a series of enclaves stretching inland which originated in coastal trading stations established between the fifteenth and eighteenth centuries. Many Portuguese and Dutch forts survive from this period, as also the old names: Grain Coast, Ivory Coast, Gold Coast and Slave Coast.

The tribes of this area are Sudanese Negroes, with many linguistic and tribal subdivisions. In physique they are tall and well-built which made them sought after as slaves for the Caribbean. This explains why the Brer Rabbit stories have so many episodes in common with African tales, even if the names of the characters are somewhat changed. Voodoo in Haiti is closely related to West African secret societies: even some names are identical. Their religion is on the whole animistic and includes ancestor cults.

Culturally some features are characteristic of this area,

such as gable-roofed huts, and a curious guitar-like instrument known as the 'West African harp.' Traditional weapons include bows, spears, swords and shields of plaited cane or similar material. Cattle and horses are rare, mainly because of the prevalent tsetse fly which also causes sleeping-sickness. The chief domestic animals are the dog, pig, goat and hen. The most cultivated crops are yams, cassava, bananas, rice, maize, millet and guinea-corn. These may be made into a kind of porridge, highly seasoned and eaten with meat, fish or vegetable gravy.

Secret societies are characteristic of this part of Africa. The Leopard societies may be little better than ritual murder-clubs, but the majority are more like Freemasons. Sometimes they are akin to professional guilds, while others act as mutual benefit clubs, enabling the poorer members to share the wealth of the richer. Others, like the Bundu or the Poro, concern themselves with the initiation of girls and boys into adult life, they maintain law and order, and regulate fishing and harvesting. Masks are commonly worn at the societies'

Both these masks, from the Baga of Guinea (l) and the Bacham of Cameroon (r), are monumental in size and conception.

ceremonies, and occur in great number and variety.

This part of Africa is noted for its skill in the plastic arts. Their carvings can be majestic, like the Baga masks, or formalized like some Ibo and Sudanese sculpture; earthily vigorous like Ashanti and Yoruba art, or suave and polished like that of the Guro. The terra-cotta heads found at Nok, in Northern Nigeria, have a radio-carbon dating to c. 250 B.C. The Ife terra-cottas and bronzes, dated to about the tenth-eleventh centuries A.D., seem to derive from the same inspiration, and tradition says that bronze-casting was brought from Ife to Benin in c. A.D. 1400 at the request of Oba Oguola of Benin. Bronze-casting at Benin continued up to the fall of Benin City in 1897, and, for tourists, to the present day. Benin bronzes are attributable on stylistic as well as traditional grounds, to three periods, and form perhaps the best-known single group of African art.

The Guinea Coast was remarkable for its number of relatively highly organized nation-states such as Ashanti, Dahomey, the Yoruba kingdoms, Benin and Nupe, all with traditional histories dating back 500 years or more. Early

Left: the dignity and humanism of this bearded ancestor mask from the Baule of the Ivory Coast make an immediate impact.

Opposite: throne of Sultan Njoya, of the Bamum tribe, Cameroon. It is of carved wood, covered with closely-strung beads.

travellers were impressed by their power and magnificence, as also by the human sacrifices practised by the Ashanti and Bini at annual harvest or ancestor-cult ceremonies. These kingdoms willingly traded with the Europeans – gold, and slaves collected from the numerous internecine wars, in return for firearms, gin, textiles, beads, and bronze manillas for currency.

Why a snake can shed its skin
(*Sierra Leone, West Africa*)

In the beginning, there was no death. Death lived with God, and at first God was unwilling to let death go into the world. But Death pleaded hard with God to be allowed to go, and at last God agreed. At the same time God made a promise to Man, that although Death had been allowed to come into the world, Man himself should not die. God also promised to send Man some new skins, which he and his family could put on when their bodies grew old.

God put the new skins into a basket, and asked the Dog to take it to Man and his family. On the way, the Dog became very hungry. Fortunately, he met some other animals who were having a big feast. So he was glad to join them, and satisfy his hunger. When he had eaten enough, he went into the shade and lay down to rest.

Among the Mende of Sierra Leone, certain officials of the women's secret society, Bundu, wear such masks over grass capes.

Soapstone *nomoli* from Sherbro, Sierra Leone, which may have been carved as an ancestor figure in the sixteenth century.

Wooden bowl from the Yoruba of Nigeria, with a sacred python, symbol of life and eternity, coiled on the lid.

While he was resting there the snake cunningly approached him and asked what he had there in his basket. So the Dog told him what was in it, and why he was carrying it to Man. Soon after that the Dog fell asleep. Then the Snake, who had been waiting nearby, picked up the basket of new skins, and slid silently away into the bush.

Soon afterwards the Dog awoke, and discovered that the Snake had stolen the basket of skins, so he ran to the Man and told him what had happened. The Man then went to God and told him about it, and demanded that the Snake should be made to return the skins. But God said that he would not take back the skins from the Snake, and that Man would have to die when he became old. From that day onwards, Man has always borne a grudge against the Snake, and has always tried to kill him whenever he sees him. The Snake, for his part, has always avoided Man, and has always lived alone. And because he still has the basket of skins that God provided, he can always shed his old skin for a new one.

Ashanti, Ghana

The first recorded visits by Portuguese travellers describe the Ashanti as a rich and powerful people. Alluvial gold dust was the staple currency (see the second of the following stories); gold ornaments enhanced the dignity of the court, while the charming brass weights used for weighing gold dust are well known. This led to the old name of that region – the Gold Coast.

How Spider obtained the Sky-God's stories
(Ashanti of Ghana, West Africa)

Kwaku Ananse, the spider, once went to Nyankonpon, the Sky-God, in order to buy the Sky-God's stories. The Sky-God said, 'What makes you think *you* can buy them?' Ananse answered, 'I know I shall be able to.' Thereupon the Sky-God said, 'Great and powerful cities like Kokofu, Bekwai, Asumengya have come, but they were unable to purchase them, and yet you, who are only a mere masterless man, you say you will be able?'

Ananse the spider said, 'What is the price of the stories?' The Sky-God said, 'They cannot be bought for anything except Onini, the python; Osebo, the leopard; Mmoatia, the fairy; and Mmoboro, the hornet.' The Spider said, 'I will bring some of all these things and what is more, I'll add my old mother Nsia (the sixth child) to the lot.'

The Sky-God said, 'Go and bring them then.' The Spider came back, and told his mother all about it, saying, 'I wish to buy the stories of the Sky-God, and he says that I must bring him Onini, the python; Osebo, the leopard; Mmoatia, the fairy; and Mmoboro, the hornet; and I said that I would add you to the lot and give you to the Sky-God in payment.'

Now Ananse the Spider consulted his wife Aso, saying, 'How shall I get Onini, the python?' Aso said to him, 'You go off and cut a branch of a palm-tree, and cut some string-creeper as well, and bring them here.' And Spider did this. Aso said, 'Take them to where the python lives.' So Ananse took them, and as he was going along, he said, 'It's longer than he is, it's not so long as he; you lie, it's longer than he.' The Spider said, 'There he is, lying over there.' The python (who had overheard this imaginary conversation) then asked,

'What's all this about?' Ananse replied, 'It is this wife of mine, Aso, who is arguing with me. She says that this palm branch is longer than you, and I say she is a liar.' So Onini, the python, said, 'Bring it, and come and measure me.' Ananse took the palm branch and laid it beside the python's body, then he said, 'Stretch yourself out.' The python stretched himself out, and Ananse took the string-creeper and wound it round and round the python and the palm-branch, and the tying was *nwenene! nwenene! nwenene!* till he came to the head, and the python was trapped.

Ananse, the spider, said, 'Fool, I shall take you to the Sky-God and receive the Sky-God's tales in return.' So Ananse

Brass goldweight, two inches high, showing a man sacrificing a white fowl to Nyame, the Sky-God, at a special altar.

21

Funerary terra-cotta head, over 100 years old, probably representing an ancestor or dead chief, from Fomena in Ashanti country, Ghana.

took him off to Nyame, the Sky-God, who said, 'My hand has touched it, it is mine; there remains what still remains.'

The Spider returned and told his wife what had happened, saying, 'There are still the hornets to catch.' His wife said, 'Look for a gourd and fill it with water and go off with it.' The Spider went along with the gourd through the bush till he saw a swarm of hornets hanging there; so he poured out some of the water and sprinkled it on them. He then poured the rest of the water over himself and cut a plantain leaf and covered his head with it. And now he spoke to the hornets, 'As the rains have come, had you better not come and take shelter in this gourd of mine so that the rains will not beat you; don't you see that I have taken a plantain leaf to cover myself?' The hornets then said, 'We thank you, we thank you,' and they all flew into the gourd, disappearing, fom! Father Spider closed the mouth of the gourd and exclaimed, 'Fools! I have got you, and I am taking you as payment for the tales of the Sky-God.'

Ananse took the hornets to the Sky-God, who said, 'My hand has touched it, it is mine; what remains, remains.'

The Spider came back, and told his wife, and said, 'There remains Osebo, the leopard.' Aso said, 'Go and dig a hole.' Ananse said, 'That's enough, I understand.' Then the Spider went off to look for the leopard's tracks, and when he had found them he dug a very deep hole in the path, covered it over, and came back home. Very early the next day, when things began to be visible, the Spider said he would go off, and when he went, lo, a leopard was lying in the pit. Ananse said, 'Little father's child, little mother's child, I have told you not to get drunk, and now, just as one would have expected, you have become intoxicated, and that's why you have fallen into the pit. If I were to say I would get you out, sure enough, the next day if you saw me or likewise any of my children, you would go and catch me and them.' The leopard said, 'Oh, I could not do a thing like that!'

Ananse then went and cut two sticks, and put one here and one there, and said, 'Put one of your paws here, and another one there.' The leopard placed his paws where he

Goldweights with animal motifs are common, and this, showing a snake catching a frog, may illustrate a proverb.

was told. As he was about to climb up out of the pit, Ananse lifted up his knife, and in a flash it descended on the leopard's head, *gao!* The pit received the leopard, and *fom!* was the sound of his fall. Ananse got a ladder, went down into the pit, got the leopard out and came back with it, exclaiming, 'Fool, I am taking you to exchange for the stories of the Sky-God.' He took the leopard to give to Nyame, the Sky-God, who said, 'My hands have touched it, it is mine; what remains, remains.'

Then the Spider came back, and carved an Akua's child, which was a flat-faced wooden doll, and he tapped some sticky latex fluid from a tree and plastered the doll's body with it. Then he made *eto* of mashed yams, and put some in the doll's hand. Again he mashed more yams, and put it in a brass basin; he tried string round the doll's waist, and took it and placed it at the foot of the odum tree, the place where the fairies come to play. And a fairy came along. She said,

—'Ananse said, "I have told you not to get drunk, . . . and that's why you have fallen into the pit." '

This stool of a chief of the Fanti, Ghana, would have been the repository of a part of his soul.

'Akua, may I eat some of this mash?' Ananse jerked the string, and the doll nodded her head. The fairy turned to one of her sisters, saying, 'She says I may eat some,' and the sister said, 'Eat some then.' And the fairy finished eating, and thanked the doll, but this time it did not answer. So the fairy said to her sister, 'When I thank her, she does not reply,' and her sister said, 'Slap her face.' The fairy slapped it, *pa!* and her hand stuck there. She told her sister, 'My hand has stuck there,' so the sister said, 'Take your other hand and slap her face again.' The fairy slapped the doll's face, *pa!* and now both her hands were stuck fast. Her sister said, 'Push it with your stomach', she did so, and her stomach stuck fast. Ananse came and tied her up, saying, 'Fool, I have got you, I shall take you to the Sky-God in exchange for his stories.' And he went off home with her.

Now Ananse spoke to his mother, Ya Nsia (the sixth child), saying, 'Come, let us go, for I am taking you along with the fairy to go and give you to the Sky-God in exchange for his stories.' He took them to where the Sky-God was sitting. When he arrived, he said, 'Sky-God, here is a fairy and also my old mother whom I spoke about.'

Then Nyame the Sky-God called his elders, the Kontire and Akwam chiefs, the Adonten, the Gyase, the Oyoko, Ankobea, and Kyidom, who were his army leaders. He put the matter before them, saying, 'Great Kings have come, and were not able to buy the Sky-God's stories, but Kwaku Ananse, the spider, has been able to pay the price: I have received from him Osebo, the leopard; I have received from him Onini, the python; I have received from him Mmoboro, the hornets; I have received from him Mmoatia, the fairy; and of his own accord, Ananse has added his own mother to the lot; all these things lie here.' Nyame said, 'Sing his praise.' '*Eee!*' they shouted. The Sky-God said, 'Kwaku Ananse, from today and going on forever, I take my Sky-God's stories and I present them to you, *kose, kose, kose,* my blessing, blessing, blessing! No more shall we call them stories of the Sky-God, but we shall call them spider-stories.'

This, my story, which I have told, if it be sweet or if it be not sweet, take some elsewhere, and let some come back to me.

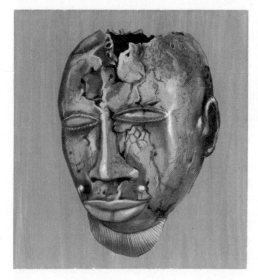

Golden trophy mask of a conquered enemy, two-thirds life size, from the treasury of King Kofi Kakari of Ashanti.

—'He met a man with a spotted dog. He said, "Show me the dog that I may buy it."'

Why Okra the cat lords it over 'Kraman the dog
(Ashanti of Ghana, West Africa)

Once upon a time there was a woman who was so unfortunate that whenever she gave birth to a child it died. So she set out to consult one of the lesser-gods about it and to tell him that she wanted a child. The lesser-god said, 'I shall give you one, but as for the child, all the work he will ever do will be to get you into debt. Nevertheless, some day he will repay you.'

It was not two days, it was not three days after consulting the lesser-god, when the woman conceived. She gave birth to a child – a spider-story child it was, for it was not long in growing up. The infant grew into a handsome youth. One day he said, 'Mother, give me gold dust that I may go to the

27

In these scales from the Ashanti there would normally be gold dust in one pan, and goldweights in the other.

Edge-of-the-Sea Country and buy salt.'

The mother said, 'How much do you want?'

He said, 'An *asuanu*'. The mother took it and gave it to him, and he set out on the journey.

Now, as he was going, he met a man with a spotted dog. He said, 'Show me the dog that I may buy it.'

The dog's master said, 'You cannot buy it.'

The youth said, 'How much is it?'

The dog's master replied, 'An *asuanu's* weight of gold dust.'

The youth said, 'What's that to me! Take this *asuanu*.' He took the dog back home, and when he returned, his mother said, 'Why did you come back so soon?'

He replied, 'I used the gold dust to buy a dog.'

His mother said, 'Ho!'

About a month later, the youth said, 'Mother, give me gold dust that I may go trading.'

She said, 'You will only take the gold dust and throw

it away again, as usual. Anyway, how much do you want?'

He replied, 'An *asuanu*-and-*suru's* worth of gold dust'.
(about £5).

The mother said, 'Take it, then.' So he set out along the
trade road. As he was going along, he met a man carrying
a cat. He said, 'Man, bring that animal that always falls on
its feet, that I may buy it.'

The man replied, 'When I lie down in my room, the mice
gnaw my feet; for that reason I bought it.'

The youth asked, 'How much will you take for it?'

Brass box for carrying gold dust, and sheet brass spoons for
measuring the gold dust onto the scales.

The man replied, 'An *asuanu*-and-*suru's* worth of gold dust.'

'So that's why you say I cannot buy it!' said the youth. 'Here, take this gold.' He received the cat and went home.

When he reached home, he said, 'Mother, look at what I have brought home.' She replied, 'Ah, that is just what they said would happen.'

About forty days later the son spoke to his mother again, saying, 'Give me gold dust that I may go trading.'

The mother said, 'All the money I have is finished except for an *asuasa's* weight of gold dust'. If I give you this, and you go, and you do not buy merchandise with it, that's the end of this business.' The boy said, 'All right'.

The next morning, when things became visible, the youth took up his bag and was off. As he was going, he met a certain Ashanti fellow who was carrying a pigeon. He said, 'Friend, show me that creature of yours that I may buy it.'

The Ashanti replied, 'I am not selling it, for I amuse myself with it.'

The youth said, 'I shall buy it.'

. . . 'Will you be able to buy it?'

. . . 'How much?'

The Ashanti replied, 'An *asuasa's* weight of gold dust.'

'Do you suppose because of that I would not buy it?' said the youth. 'Here is the gold.'

The youth brought the bird home. His mother said, 'This has turned out no better than before. So this is what you have brought?' He replied, 'All the same, this is what I have brought.'

Now one day the boy was living there at home, when the pigeon called to him. When he went to it, the pigeon spoke to him, saying, 'In my own village I am a chief, and I was about to go on a journey when a certain fellow came and caught me. Then you, out of your kindness, bought me, and now I implore you to bring me back to my own town where the people will thank you greatly.'

'You are telling me lies,' said the youth. 'You will run away.'

—'His mother said, "This has turned out no better than before. So this is what you have brought?"'

The pigeon said, 'If that's what you are afraid of, take a string and tie it to my leg, and take me along.'

The youth took a string and fastened it to the pigeon's leg, and it followed behind him till they arrived at the pigeon's town.

There they got a hammock and the regalia and brought the chief to his house. The whole tribe was told the news – how he was setting out on a journey, and how a certain fellow had caught him, and how this youth by his kindness had bought him, and how today he had brought him home.

The elders and the young people all stood and thanked the youth. The queen mother brought a waterpot full of gold dust, and all of the elders each gave a waterpot full of gold dust as well. The chief himself looked on his hand and slipped off a ring and gave it to the youth, saying, 'Take this ring, and it will give you whatever you desire.'

'I have heard,' said the youth and he went off with the ring to his village, and showed the gold dust and the ring to his mother.

Then the mother said, 'Welcome! Welcome!' Formerly, when the youth, having squandered his gold dust and returned from his journeys, would salute his mother, she used not to answer him. He told his mother the news, saying, 'You have seen this gold dust and this ring; I shall go and build a great village for us to live in.'

The youth set out and went and stood in the bush. He slipped off the ring and placed it on the ground and said, 'Ring, clear all this land of forest and bush for me.' And the whole of the place became cleared. He said, 'Collect all which you have cleared into heaps for burning.' And it did so. He said, 'Build houses.' And it built many houses. He said, 'Ring, let people come and live in these houses.' And people came.

The youth made his mother queen mother and he became chief.

Now Ananse, the spider, was his best friend. One day, when the youth was living there in his new home, Kwaku

The Asantehene, or King of the Ashanti, is a splendid figure in full regalia, with attendants all around.

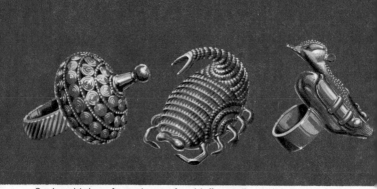

Such gold rings formed part of a chief's regalia, and the magic ring may have been of this sort.

Ananse set out to visit this village. When he reached it, he exclaimed, 'Oh, little mother's child, little father's child, you have been fortunate and successful and you don't care any more about me or to look after me. But what has happened to bring all this about?'

Then the youth told him everything. The spider said, 'I shall go to my village to get something and return.'

Ananse went off to his village. He said to his niece, 'I shall send you to my friend over there, and when you go you will take this wine for him, and flatter him, and do whatever he orders, and you must try secretly to get hold of that ring.'

The girl set out and went to the youth's village. The youth insisted that she should stay with him for three days before returning home. One day the youth went to bathe. He slipped off the ring and laid it on a table, and the girl took it and went off to her uncle, Kwaku Ananse. As soon as Ananse the spider laid hands on it, he made use of it to build a big town.

Now, the youth, when he came to look for his ring, could not find it. He came to hear that the spider had built a big town which was greater than his own. So he went off to consult one of the lesser-gods. The lesser-god told him, 'Ananse's niece who visited you has taken your ring and given it to her uncle.' The spider also went to consult a lesser-god, and it was revealed to him that Okra, the cat, and 'Kraman, the dog, would be sent to recover the ring. So he went and got medicine with which to dope some meat he intended to place on the path, so that when the animals came that way, if they ate some of the meat, they would be unable to go on at all.

The youth who had lost his ring came home and told the cat and the dog: 'The time has now come for me to tell you the reason why I bought you, and it is this: a ring belonging to me has been lost, and they say the spider has it, but that it is in a box which is in the middle of all the rest of his boxes. They say he has mixed medicine with mutton and placed it on the path. So when you come to it, don't eat it, but jump over.'

The dog said, 'Cat, have you heard? You are the one who will chew it.'

'Oh, go along!' said the cat, 'you who every little while take your nose to sniff and sniff!'

Then they began to bicker, and their master said, 'That's all right, be off.'

Spiders occur fairly rarely in African art, but in this 'spider stool' from Cameroon they form an effective openwork design.

—'The cat took a string and tied it around the mouse's middle. Then the mouse went into the spider's room.'

The two animals set out and were going along the path. They were quite near the place where the meat was, when the dog smelt it. He said, 'Cat, I have a pain in my stomach and I can't go on.'

The cat said, 'Come, come! Let us go on, we are on important business.'

The dog said, 'Cat, I can't possibly.'

The cat went on alone. The dog then went to where the meat was, and he ate it all up. There he lay! He was unable to go any further. And the cat reached Ananse's village, and lay down on the rafters above Ananse's room. As he lay there, he saw a mouse passing and caught it at once. The mouse said, 'Don't kill me, what do you want?'

The cat replied, 'My master's ring has been lost and they say it lies in Ananse's box, which stands in the middle of all the rest of his boxes. If you are able to fetch the ring from Ananse's box for me, I will let you go.'

Brass *kuduo* from the Ashanti which, containing gold dust and beads to 'wash the soul', was buried with its owner.

'. . . I can do it.'

The cat said, 'Suppose I release you, and instead of bringing the ring, you run away?'

'If you wish, fasten a string round my middle,' said the mouse.

The cat took a string and tied it around the mouse's middle. Then the mouse went off into the spider's room and gnawed a hole in the box which stood in the middle of all the rest. He went into the box, got the ring, and brought it to the cat. No sooner did the cat lay hands on it, then he ran off homewards, and came across the dog, who was lying near where the meat had been. The cat said, 'You are still lying here! And where is the meat?'

The dog said, 'Oh, I did not see what became of it. Perhaps the people who owned it came and removed it. But have you the ring?' 'Here it is,' said the cat. The dog said, 'They say that the river which we must cross is in flood, and as you, Cat, walk

37

Akua'ba doll carried by girls as a charm to ensure beautiful children. Small gourd stamps print the pattern on the cloth.

on the bottom when you cross the water, the ring might fall down, so you had better give it to me, for as you know, I swim on the surface of the water.'

'That's true,' said the cat. 'You take it.'

They reached the river, the dog jumped in and so did the cat, who crossed over at once. The dog got half way over and became tired and, as he was about to take a deep breath, the ring fell out of his mouth into the water. He rejoined the cat.

The cat said, 'Where is that ring?' The dog said, 'It fell out of my mouth into the water.' The cat ran into the river; he saw a great fish passing and caught it. The fish said, 'What is it?'

The cat said, 'My ring has just fallen into this river, so unless you want trouble, give it back to me at once. Otherwise I shall kill you immediately.'

The fish said, 'Let us go to the river bank that I may return it to you.' When they both reached the bank, the fish vomited and the ring came out.

The cat took it and came and showed it to the dog. The dog said, 'Father, I beg of you, don't speak about what has happened.' But the cat remained silent. They reached home, and the cat told his master all that had happened.

All the people who were present praised the cat.

Then the chief said, 'You, Cat, whatever kind of food I am eating, I will see to it that I break some and place it in your little dish. Whatever mat I sleep upon, I shall only lie upon it provided you lie on some of it. As for you, Dog, you will only lie on the smouldering embers of the dead fire when the chilly night comes. And people will flog you.'

That is why you will always see the cat sleeping nowhere but on the best mat; also, if you throw some food on to the ground for him, he will not eat it, but eat only from a plate. But as for the dog – we shall always see him sleeping in the courtyard on the dead ashes of the day's fire; also you will see him there being beaten, and yelping *'Kao!'*

It is all because of the time when the cat and the dog were sent on this business of the ring.

This, my story, which I have told, if it be sweet, or if it be not sweet, some you may take as true, and the rest you may praise me for my telling of it.

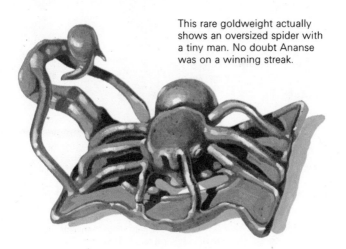

This rare goldweight actually shows an oversized spider with a tiny man. No doubt Ananse was on a winning streak.

Southern Nigerian tribes

The three principal tribal groups of Nigeria are the Hausa, the Yoruba, and the Ibo.

The Yoruba, living west of the Niger, are a united, urbanized people. Ife, still their religious capital, dates back to at least the tenth century A.D.

East of the Niger, the Ibo, rivals of the Yoruba, are the chief tribe. There are numerous sub-tribes and smaller tribes.

Benin, famous for its bronzes, iron work and carved ivory, is independent of these three main tribal groups, though influenced in the distant past by the Yoruba.

Nigerian tribal art is exceedingly rich and varied, mostly consisting of woodcarvings, but gold, bronze and brass, ivory and beadwork are also used in their sculpture.

Tortoise and the wisdom of the world
(Nigeria, West Africa)
Once upon a time, the Tortoise, who was ambitious, thought that he would like to possess all the wisdom in the whole world, and be the only wise person in the world. If

Above: wooden verandah posts, from the residence of the king of Savé, Dahomey, representing the gods Odudua and Obatala.

Opposite: this turtle, about two inches long, on a bronze vase from Benin, beautifully combines formalized pattern with naturalistic shape.

he succeeded in this ambition he would then be so wise that everybody, including great kings and aged councillors, would have to consult him whenever they wanted to solve any problem, however small. He thought, too, that perhaps he could charge a great deal of money for giving his advice.

He set out to collect all the wisdom in the world, and as he gathered each piece he put it into a large gourd, the opening of which he stopped up tightly with a roll of leaves. This took a long time, and when Tortoise thought he had collected all there was, he decided to hide the gourd of wisdom on top of a very high tree which no one else could climb.

When he got to the tree he tied a rope to the neck of the gourd, and tied the two ends together, and put the loop over his head, thereby hanging the gourd from his neck so that it rested on his stomach. He tried to climb the tree, but found that he could not for the gourd kept getting in his way. He went on trying for some time, putting the gourd to one side of his stomach or trying to stretch past it, but his efforts to climb the tree were all in vain. As he stood at the bottom of the tree, wondering what to do next, he heard somebody behind him laughing heartily. He turned round and saw a hunter, who had been watching him.

'Friend,' said the hunter, 'why don't you hang that

gourd behind you if you want to get to the top of that tree?'

On hearing this piece of common-sense advice, and realizing that there was at least that much wisdom left in a world which he thought he had deprived of all wisdom, Tortoise was so frustrated at the hopelessness of his task that he dropped the gourd of wisdom then and there at the bottom of the tree and broke it. After that the wisdom of the world was scattered in little pieces everywhere, and anyone can find a little of it if they search hard enough.

Why the sun and the moon live in the sky
(Efik-Ibibio tribe, Nigeria, West Africa)

Many years ago the sun and the water were great friends, and both lived on the earth. The sun often visited the place where the water lived, but the water never returned his visits. One day, the sun asked the water: 'Why do you and your relations never come to visit me? We would be very pleased to see you in our compound.'

The water replied, 'I'm sorry, but your compound is not big enough, and if I visited you with all my people, I

A cubistic statuette from the Ibo of Nigeria, $6\frac{1}{2}$ inches high.

Opposite: (upper) wooden mask from the Yoruba, forty inches high, showing two mothers each with two children.

(lower) Ibo mask of the beautiful, gentle Maiden Spirit, which dances with a mask of the ugly, robust Elephant Spirit.

42

would be afraid of driving you and your wife away. If you really wish me to visit you,' the water continued, 'you must build a very large compound, and I warn you that it will have to be a tremendous place as my people and I take up so much room, and if it is not big enough we might damage your property.'

The sun promised to build a very big compound, and soon afterwards he returned home to his wife, the moon. The sun told his wife what he had promised the water and the very next day he began to build a truly enormous compound in which to entertain his friend.

When it was completed, the sun asked the water to visit him the very next day.

The water arrived, and before coming in he called out to the sun, asking if he was really sure that the compound was large enough, and the sun answered, 'Yes, come in, my friend.'

The water then began to flow in, accompanied by the fish and all the water animals.

Very soon the water was knee-deep, so he asked the sun if it was still safe, and the sun said, 'Yes,' so even more water came in.

When the water was level

with the top of a man's head, he again asked the sun, 'Are you really sure you want me and my people to come?'

The sun and the moon both answered, 'Yes,' not knowing any better, so the water continued to flow in, till at last the sun and the moon had to climb on to the roof to keep dry.

Again the water asked, 'Do you still want my people and me to come into your compound?' and the sun, not liking to go back on his word, insisted, 'Yes, let them all come.'

Soon the water flowed over the very top of the roof, and the sun and the moon were forced to go up into the sky, where they have lived ever since.

How a hunter cheated his friends
(Efik-Ibibio tribe, Nigeria, West Africa)

Many years ago there was a Calabar hunter named Effiong who lived in the bush. He killed plenty of animals and made much money. Every one in the country knew him, and one of his best friends was a man called Okun, who lived near him.

Effiong was very extravagant and spent so much money in eating and drinking with everyone that at last he became quite poor, and he had to go out hunting again. But now his good luck seemed to have left him, for although he worked hard and hunted by night and by day, he completely failed to catch anything.

One day, as he was very hungry, he went to his friend Okun and borrowed two hundred rods of money from him. He told Okun to come to his house on a certain day for repayment of this money, and he also told him to bring his gun, loaded, with him.

Now, some time before this, Effiong had made friends with a leopard and a bush cat whom he had met in the forest while on one of his hunting expeditions; and he had also made friends with a goat and a cock at a farm where he had stayed for the night. But, though Effiong had borrowed all this money from Okun, he had no idea how he was going to repay it on the day he had promised. At last, however, he thought of a plan.

The next day he went to his friend the leopard and asked him to lend him two hundred rods of money, promising to return this sum on the same day as he had promised to repay

Right: small Yoruba ivory carving of a horseman. The form of the horse is dictated by the diameter of the tusk.

Below: formerly attributed to Benin, this bronze figure of a huntsman returning with an antelope over his shoulders is vigorously imaginative.

This bronze plaque of a huntsman aiming at an ibis in a tree is a very informal composition by Benin standards.

Okun. He also told the leopard that, if he were absent when he came for the money, he could kill anything he saw in the house and eat it. The leopard was then to wait until Effiong arrived, when he would repay him the money. To this the leopard agreed.

The hunter then went to his friend the goat and borrowed two hundred rods from him in the same way. He also went to his friends the bush cat and the cock and borrowed two hundred rods from each of them on the same conditions, and told each one of them that if he were absent when they arrived, they could kill and eat anything they found about the place.

When the day appointed for the repayment of these debts arrived, Effiong spread some corn on the ground, and then slipped away and left the house deserted. Very early in the morning, soon after he had begun to crow, the cock remembered what the hunter had told him, and he walked over to the hunter's house but found no one there. On looking around, however, he saw some corn on the ground and, being hungry, he started to eat.

About this time the bush cat also arrived, and not seeing the hunter around, he too looked about, and very soon he saw the cock who was busy pecking at the corn. So the bush cat crept up behind and pounced on the cock, killing him at once, and began to eat him.

By this time the goat had come for his money, but, failing to find the hunter, he walked about until he came upon the bush cat who was so intent on his meal off the cock that he

Bronze and gilt hip pendant of a type worn by the Oba, or ruler of Benin, Southern Nigeria.

did not notice the goat approaching; and the goat, who was in rather a bad temper at having to wait for his money, at once charged at the bush cat and butted him with his horns, knocking him over. The bush cat did not like this at all, so, as he was not big enough to fight the goat, he picked up the remains of the cock and ran off with it into the bush; and so he forfeited his money by not awaiting the hunter's arrival. The goat was thus left all alone and started bleating. This noise attracted the attention of the leopard, who was on his way to receive his payment from the hunter. As the leopard got nearer, the smell of goat became very strong and being ravenous, for he had not eaten anything for some time, he approached stealthily. Not seeing the hunter about, he stalked the goat very carefully.

Meanwhile, the goat was quietly grazing, quite unsuspicious of any danger as he was in the compound of his friend the hunter. Now and then he said, 'Baa!' But most of the time he was busy eating the young grass and picking up the leaves which had fallen from a tree of which he was very fond. Suddenly the leopard sprang at the goat and, with one crunch at the neck, brought him down. The goat was killed at once, and the leopard started on his meal.

It was now about eight o'clock in the morning, and Okun, the hunter's friend, having breakfasted, went out with his gun to collect the two hundred rods that Effiong owed him. When he got close to the house he heard a crunching sound. Being a hunter himself, he approached cautiously, and, looking over the fence, he saw the leopard only a few yards off, busily eating the goat. So he aimed carefully and fired, and the leopard rolled over dead.

With the leopard's death, four of the hunter's creditors were now disposed of, as the bush cat had killed the cock; the goat had driven the bush cat away, who thus forfeited his claim; and in his turn the goat had been killed by the leopard, who had just been shot by Okun. This meant a saving of eight hundred rods to Effiong, but this did not satisfy him. As soon as he heard the report of the gun, he ran out and found the leopard lying dead with Okun standing over it. Then Effiong began to upbraid Okun and asked him why he had killed the leopard. He said that he would report the whole matter to the King. Okun became frightened and begged him not to say anything about the matter, as the King would be angry; but the hunter insisted that he would tell the King. At last Okun said, 'If you will leave the whole matter alone and say no more about it, I will make you a present of the two hundred rods you borrowed from me.' This was just what Effiong wanted, and he agreed, and told Okun to go and that he would bury the body of his friend the leopard.

But as soon as Okun had gone, Effiong dragged the leopard's body into the house, and skinned it very carefully. When the skin was well cured, the hunter took it to a distant market where he sold it for much money.

And now, whenever a bush cat sees a cock he always kills it and does so by right, as he takes the cock in part payment of the two hundred rods which the hunter never paid him.

Moral: Never lend money to people, because if they cannot pay they will try to kill you or get rid of you in some way, either by poison or by setting bad *jujus* for you.

These figures of dried clay on a cane framework are made by the Ibo of Eastern Nigeria for the Mbari festival.

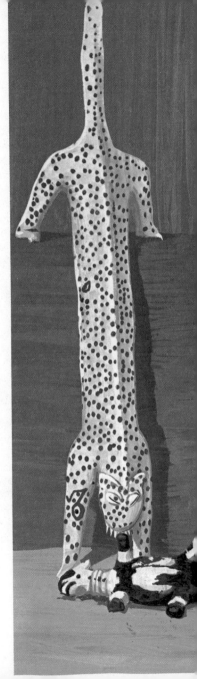

Bag of goatskin or 'morocco' leather, made by the Northern Nigerian Hausa. Appliqué and decorative stitching give a striking polychrome effect.

Opposite: this, the oldest surviving mosque in West Africa, is built out of sun-dried bricks, and is the principal mosque of Timbuktu.

Hausa tribes

The term 'Hausa' has a three-fold connotation: a) language b) the country where the main body of Hausa-speaking peoples live, and c) Hausawa, or all those peoples of the Central and Western Sudan who speak Hausa.

The language is a *lingua franca* for the interior of West Africa, as Swahili is in East Africa. This is doubtless due to the trading activities of both groups of people, and many words derive from Arabic. The Hausa themselves believe that they originated somewhere east of Mecca. They have had their own Arabic writing for 150 years if not longer, and are the only people in tropical Africa to have done this themselves. Their literature includes historical epics and poetry.

Hausaland takes up most of Northern Nigeria and historically comprises seven states named after the seven sons of the legendary founder. In the Middle Ages they were very powerful, but by 1810 they were conquered by the Fulani.

The Hausa people themselves are classified as Sudanese negroes. They are very black and physically strong, which they attribute to their diet – mainly guinea-corn porridge with a lot of red pepper, as against the yam and banana staple of other Nigerian tribes.

In religion the Hausa are predominantly Moslem. Islam is not very strictly observed in West Africa, partly because there the month-long Ramadan fast, with total abstinence between sunrise and sunset, is a real ordeal. Many make the pilgrimage to Mecca, taking five to six years over it, and combining it with business. In fact, the Hausa are the chief traders of Nigeria and form an important link between the trans-Saharan trade and the areas to the south. Kano, Katsina and Sokoto are the main trading centres.

The great Islamic empires that fringed the southern Sahara in the Middle Ages have left their mark. Hausa architecture is of a type found as far west as Timbuktu and Jenne. The high-walled buildings with towers and crenellations are made of sun-dried bricks made of mud mixed with straw, the same material being used for mortar and rendering. Possible survivals from the days of the Crusades and Knights Templar include cavalry with armour of quilting and chain mail and two-handed swords, who indulge in ceremonial charges and combats.

The influence of Islam has meant that representational art occurs chiefly among the pagan tribes. The charming 'tandu' animal figures are almost the only exception, but artistic skill is apparent in their leather, basketry and weaving.

Decoration in white chain-stitch for the front of a Hausa robe, which is made of many narrow strips sewn together.

How Spider escaped Death

(Hausa Tribes, West Africa)

Once upon a time Death was walking about the country. He was looking for victims, and as a bait, he led behind him a very fat ox. He only asked one price – that after a year had gone by the purchaser should not forget his name. If he should forget his name, then Death would carry him off. Now Spider was poor and starving with no idea where the next meal was going to come from, and of course he hastened to buy the fat ox at that price.

After Spider had bought the ox and had agreed with Death upon the price – that he must be able to repeat Death's name, Wanabéri, at the end of a year – he led the beast home in triumph. There he killed it and skinned it and cut it into pieces for the members of his family, and their time of hunger was passed.

Death went on his way, and Spider called his wife and his son, and ordered them to sing this new song every day while working: 'Wanakiri, Wanabéri.' By this means Spider hoped

'Death . . . was looking for his victims, and as a bait, he led behind him a very fat ox.'

—'Wait! the child cried out, and he rushed to a tree, climbed very
high . . . and cried out, "Wanakiri, Wanabéri!"'

to fix Death's name in their memory so that it would not be
forgotten.

For six months, no other song was heard in that household.
It pounded with the pestle crushing the millet, it blew with
the fan winnowing the husk from the grain. That song accompanied the jug to draw water at the well, it heard all the
stories of the village, and returned home between the high
walls of the compound. It went to the fields with the women
in the morning, and kept time with the hoe tending the rows
of maize or millet or digging the sweet potato. And in the evening the same song rocked the child and lulled him to sleep.

But the seventh month came, and only one word was left of
the song.

In the eighth month there was only a tune.

By the ninth month it was only as dust in dust.

But at last the twelfth month came. There came the last day
of the twelfth month, the three hundred and sixty-fifth day

of the year and finally the last hour and the last minute of that day.

Then suddenly, there came a knock at the door.

Spider called out, 'Who is there?'

Back came the grim answer: 'It is I, Death. Can you tell me my name?'

'One moment!' cried Spider in panic. 'It is hidden in my granary!' Quickly he ran to his wife. 'That song I told you to sing! Do you remember it? What is Death's name?'

Spider's wife had forgotten, but any answer was better than no answer, so she told him, 'Dindin-Dingouna!'

Spider was greatly relieved, went back to the door where Death was waiting, and repeated, 'Dindin-Dingouna!'

'Oh indeed! So you call that my name?' cried Death in fury and triumph, and he snatched up Spider and strode off, carrying him away.

In the yard the wife was weeping bitterly as she realized what her forgetfulness had led to. Her son asked what the matter was, and she told him.

'Wait!' the child cried, and he rushed to a tree, climbed as high as he could, saw Death going away and carrying off his father and cried out, 'Wanakiri! Wanabéri!'

Spider was saved, and Death went away.

Every good son knows there may be debts to pay after the death of his father.

Flat baskets such as these are used by the Hausa as trays for their bread, which resembles pancakes or *chapatis*.

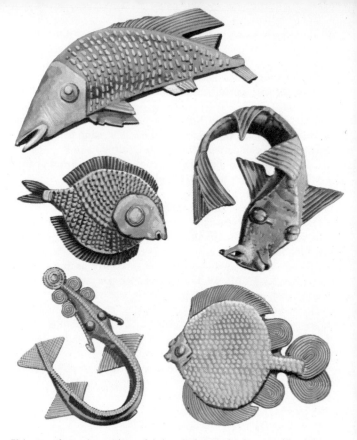

Fish are a favourite subject of Ashanti *cire-perdue* brass goldweights, and come in a variety of shapes and sizes.

The Spider, the Elephant, and the Hippopotamus
(Hausa Tribes, West Africa)

Once upon a time there was a famine, the crops failed, and both by land and by water there was no food to be had. Spider and his family had finished all their store of food, and were beginning to feel the pains of starvation. So one day he went to see Elephant. 'God give you long life,' said Spider. 'Sarkin Ruwa, the hippopotamus, has sent me to visit you. He says that if you will let him have a hundred baskets of corn now, he will give you a fine stallion when harvest comes round. But he insists that this agreement is to be just between you two great ones, and that no one else must hear of it.'

'Fair enough,' said Elephant, and he gave orders for one hundred baskets of corn to be brought out. The young elephants picked them up and carried them to the water's edge.

'Put them down here,' said Spider. 'You've done more than your share of the work and can go home now. I will get Hippopotamus to send his young men to collect the stuff. It will be quite all right here. No one else will take it.'

As soon as the young elephants had gone, Spider called his wife and children, and together they carried all the corn home and stored it away.

Next morning, Spider went down to the river's edge and down into the water to the bottom of the river. He made his way to Hippopotamus's palace, passed through his courtiers and entered the private rooms. Here he bowed deeply to Hippopotamus and said, 'God give the chief long life.'

'Amen to that,' said Hippopotamus. 'Well, Gizo, where have you come from and what business brings you here?'

'I come to act as go-between,' said Spider. 'Sarkin Tudu, the elephant, has sent me with a message for you. He wishes me to tell you that he has plenty of corn for making dumplings but nothing tasty to eat with them. So he wants you to let him have one hundred baskets of fish now, and then when harvest time comes round he will give you a stallion.'

'That seems a fair bargain,' said Hippopotamus.

'He also says that this is an arrangement just between you two great ones,' added Spider, 'and that you must on no account tell any one else about it.'

'All right', said Hippopotamus and with that he gave orders for one hundred baskets of fish to be collected. The young hippopotamuses brought them up to the river bank and put them down there.

'You can go now,' said Spider. 'I'll go and call the young elephants to collect them and take them to Elephant's palace.'

'But if we leave them here,' said the young hippos, 'what happens if somebody else comes and takes them?'

'Don't you worry about that,' said Spider. 'No one will touch them here. But we simply can't have the young men of two

—'It went on like that all day with the elephants pulling at one end, and the hippos pulling at the other end.'

different chiefs congregating in the same place. If you were to stay around here until the young elephants turned up, goodness only knows what bickering there would be between you. And then perhaps you would set your chiefs against one another. Truly,' Spider continued, 'they say it's young men who eat the beans, but the elders who get the belly-ache.'

'That's true,' said the eldest of the young hippos. 'We had better go home.'

When they had gone, Spider called his wife and children again, and together they picked up all the fish, carried it home, dried it in the sun and stored it away. Now Spider and his family had no more anxiety about food.

From that time until harvest-time Spider kept all his family busy plaiting rope. When the time for harvest came round, they had made a rope which was very very long and very very strong.

Then one day, after the harvest had been gathered, and after the bush had been burnt in readiness for the sowing, Elephant remembered the agreement and said, 'Go and fetch

Spider.' And so Spider was brought in front of Elephant.

'Well, Gizo,' said Elephant. 'Is Hippopotamus doing anything about that agreement you made between us?'

'I'm sure you don't need to worry,' said Spider. 'I'll go right
away and see him about it and be back the day after tomorrow.'

So Spider went off and was away for three days. But what
he really did was to go to the river bank, where he marked
down an enormous tree, and tied the middle part of his rope
round the trunk. Then he came back to Elephant bringing
with him one end of the rope. He said, 'Here's the tethering-
rope of the stallion which Hippopotamus is giving you. At
daybreak tomorrow they will bring him out of the water, and
they say that as soon as you see the leaves of that tree over
there shaking, your young men are to pull on the rope.'

'So that's how it is to be,' said the Elephant.

'Yes,' said Spider.

'Well,' said the Elephant, 'God bring us tomorrow.'

'Amen to that,' said Spider.

After that Spider went to see Hippopotamus, taking with
him the other end of the rope.

The Ibo man who made this painted clay figure of an elephant for the Mbari festival had obviously never seen one.

'Elephant has given me a stallion to bring to you,' he said, but I'm not strong enough to hold him and so I've left him tied up to a tree on the bank. Here's the other end of the tethering-rope. You had better send out your young men at daybreak to pull him in, but look out, he's very wild and very strong.'

'All right,' said Hippopotamus, 'we'll do that.'

The next morning, at daybreak, Elephant had all his young men lined up holding the rope, at the ready. As soon as the young hippos began to pull on the rope, the tree shook as if it was coming up by the roots, and at that the young elephants started hauling as well. It went on like that all day with the elephants pulling at one end and the hippos pulling at the other end. If the elephants gained any ground, the hippos put more men on the rope and if the hippos gained any ground, the elephants did the same. They pulled and they tugged, and they tugged and they pulled, and it was not till nightfall that the two teams stopped to lie down and rest.

At daybreak the next morning, they got up and started pulling again, the elephants at one end of Spider's rope, the hippos at the other. Again the two teams tugged and hauled; and at last, when it was midday, Hippopotamus told his young men to stop. 'Go and ask Elephant,' he said, 'what kind of horse this is that he has given me.'

At the same moment, Elephant was telling his young men to stop pulling and go and ask Hippopotamus what kind of horse he had given them. So both parties of young men set off, and it so happened that they met together.

'Where are you off to?' asked the young elephants.

'We have been sent to speak to the old Elephant,' explained the young hippos, 'to ask what kind of horse it is that he has given our Chief in settlement for one hundred baskets of fish. We have been pulling at that creature's rope all day yesterday and since daybreak today and we are utterly worn out.'

'But that's impossible!' exclaimed the young elephants. 'We

Lidded bowl from the Hausa, Northern Nigeria, made from a gourd cut in two halves, with pokerwork decoration.

have been sent to speak to the old Hippopotamus, to ask him what kind of horse it is that he has given our Chief in settlement for one hundred baskets of corn. He promised us a stallion, and we have been pulling at its rope all yesterday and since daybreak today till there is no strength left in us.'

The two parties of young men argued like this for a while, and almost came to blows, but at last they realized that the old Elephant and the old Hippopotamus had not met when they made this agreement, and that it was Spider who had been the go-between, and that Spider had made away with the hundred baskets of corn and the hundred baskets of fish.

'Well, if that's how things are,' they decided, 'we'd better go back and say that there's no horse here and that this looks like one of Spider's tricks.' And so both parties of young men went back and told what had happened and what they guessed Spider had been doing.

Brer Rabbit, the cunning African Hare, is clearly shown in this mask from the Yoruba of Nigeria.

'But I don't owe Hippopotamus anything,' protested Elephant when he heard the news. 'It is he who is in debt to me.'

'I'm not in debt to Elephant,' said Hippopotamus. 'It's the other way round.'

But at last the old Elephant and the old Hippopotamus realized that Spider had tricked them and had taken all their food. Hippopotamus accordingly sent a message to Elephant to say that they must not be angry with each other. 'After all,' he said, 'we are among the great ones of the world, and if we fall out, the quarrel will not easily be repaired. Instead, it would be as well for us to lie in wait and catch that Spider who has tricked us out of so much food.'

Elephant agreed with the wisdom of this, and from then on both of them started hunting the Spider. But neither the Elephant or the Hippopotamus were able to find him anywhere because Spider stayed in hiding till he was quite thin again.

This mask from the Nupe of Northern Nigeria, a Moslem tribe, is a rare surviving example of their representational art.

63

The Rabbit, the Elephant, and the Giraffe

(Hausa Tribes, West Africa).

One day Rabbit suggested to Elephant that they should do some farming together. 'You can clear the bush and I'll burn the trees when you have pushed them over.' Elephant agreed and began pushing trees over to clear the land.

Rabbit next went to Giraffe and made the same suggestion to him. 'I'll push over the trees,' said Rabbit, 'and you can burn them.' Giraffe agreed, and went and burnt all the trees which Elephant had already pushed over. Rabbit, of course, just took care that neither Elephant nor Giraffe knew what the other was doing.

When the first rains fell, Rabbit went to see Elephant. 'Giwa,' he said, 'you do the sowing and I will do the hoeing.'

Later on he went to see Giraffe. 'Rakumin Dawa,' he said, 'I've done the sowing and now it's your turn to do the hoeing.'

Still later on, when the corn was ripe, Rabbit went back to Elephant. 'Now, Giwa,' he said, 'if you go and reap, I will gather it.'

When Elephant had done the reaping, Rabbit went back to

Giraffe. 'I've finished the reaping,' said he, 'and now it's all ready for you to gather.'

Finally, after all the work had been done, Rabbit went to see Elephant again. 'Well, Giwa,' he said, 'the corn's all gathered and ready, so let's bring it in tomorrow. There's just one thing I should warn you though,' he continued, 'I've heard there's a creature called Giraffe that's going to try and take it off us.'

'Who or what is Giraffe?' asked Elephant. 'Well, never mind, I'm big enough to cope with most things. We'll deal with it tomorrow. Good night, now.'

Rabbit went straight from Elephant to Giraffe. 'I say, Rakumin Dawa,' he called, 'I've just heard about a creature called Elephant. They say he's going to try and steal our corn.'

'Who or what is Elephant?' snorted Giraffe. 'Don't worry about it now, we'll deal with him tomorrow.'

Next day Giraffe was up early and was the first to arrive at the farm. When Rabbit arrived a few moments later, Giraffe said, 'Look here, Zomo, where's that Elephant you said was coming to steal our corn?'

— 'So off charged Elephant to the east . . . the Giraffe lost no time at all, but galloped off to the west.'

'He'll soon be here, I expect,' said Rabbit. 'Look, there he is now,' he added, as Elephant appeared. 'Do you see him?'

'Where?' asked Giraffe. 'Over by that hill?'

'That's no hill,' said Rabbit. 'That is Elephant!'

'Mercy on us!' exclaimed Giraffe. 'I can't take him on!'

'All right,' said Rabbit, 'if you can't you'd better hide. Lie down here, stretch your neck along the ground, and lie quite still.'

Giraffe lost no time in doing as he was told, and Rabbit crossed over to Elephant. 'Hey, Zomo,' said Elephant, 'where's that Giraffe you said was going to take our corn?'

'He was here early waiting for you,' said Rabbit, 'but he's gone off for a swim. That's his guitar over there,' he added, pointing to Giraffe's outstretched neck.

'Good Lord!' said Elephant. 'If that's his guitar he's a bigger beast than I can tackle.'

'Well then, Giwa,' said Rabbit, 'if you feel you can't take him on you'd better run for it before he comes back.'

So off charged Elephant towards the east. Rabbit then went back to Giraffe, and said, 'He's going over to the east looking for you, Rakumin Dawa. You'd better clear out while the going's good before he comes back and finds you.' The Giraffe immediately jumped up and galloped off to the west.

So Rabbit was left with all that corn. He took it back to his house and after that he lived a life of leisure.

Dan-Kano and Dan-Katsina
(Hausa Tribes, West Africa)

There were once two sharp-witted rogues who lived by trickery, one of whom came from Kano, the other from Katsina.

One day the rogue from Kano peeled the bark off a baobab tree and took it to the dye-pits, and dyed it blue and beat it to give it a glaze, and finally wrapped it up in paper to look like the best blue broadcloth.

While the rogue from Kano was doing this, the rogue from Katsina was filling a goatskin with pebbles. When he had finished doing that, he covered the top of the pebbles over with a couple of hundred cowries, tied up the bag, and set out for the market.

Seventeenth-century Benin bronze figure of a horseman, whose feathered headdress shows that he came from Northern Nigeria.

On the way to the market the two rogues happened to meet, and fell into conversation together.

'Where are you going to, my friend?' asked the Kano man.

'I'm going to market,' said the Katsina man. 'Is that where you are going? And what have you got to sell?'

'Best blue broadcloth,' said the Kano man.

'Fancy that! That's just what I was going to market to buy,' answered the Katsina man. 'I've got my money here,' he went on, pointing to the goatskin bag, 'in cowries, twenty thousand of them.'

To cut a long story short, the two rogues struck a bargain on the spot and exchanged their wares long before they reached the market. They parted company in great friendship, since each thought he had got the better of the other, and when they had gone on a short distance, they each turned aside to see what sort of a bargain they had got. Of course, the Kano man found that he had got a bag of stones, and the Katsina man found that he had been fobbed off with a parcel of bark.

At this they both turned back and retraced their steps, and when they met again they said, 'We are each as crafty as the other, so from now on we had better join forces and seek our fortune together.'

So the two rogues became partners and took to the road. When they came to a town they equipped themselves with water-bottles and staffs and begging-bowls, and then, pretending to be blind beggars, they set off again.

They were going along the road, deep in the bush, when they came to a place where a party of traders had pitched their camp. They did not let the traders see them, however, but hid in the undergrowth near the camp.

When night was falling, and the traders were settling down to their evening meal, the two rogues came out of hiding and entered the traders' camp with their eyes closed, pretending to be blind beggars. The traders were quite taken in by this masquerade, gave them some food, let them stay in the camp, and in due course went to sleep. But as soon as they were all asleep the two rogues opened their eyes and removed all the traders' goods and carried them over to a dry well into which they dropped them.

—'Then he went back to . . . the pile of stones and started hurling them down into the well.'

Early the next day the traders woke and found they had been robbed of everything. While they were searching around for traces of the robbers and lamenting their losses, the two rogues awoke. Hearing what was going on, they also got up and started groping about, saying, 'Where are our water-bottles? Let's hope they haven't been stolen.' This made the traders very angry. 'Here we are,' they cried, 'robbed of all we have, and all you miserable beggars can think about is whether your water-bottles have been taken as well. Get out of here before we throw you out.' So the two rogues groped their way out of the traders' camp and went into hiding close by.

Soon afterwards the traders left, loudly bewailing their misfortune in being robbed. As soon as they had gone the two rogues made sure the coast was clear, and then hurried over to the well where the stolen goods were hidden.

'Dan-Katsina,' said the Kano man, 'you go down.'

'No, Dan-Kano,' said Dan-Katsina, 'you go.'

'No, you,' said Dan-Kano.

So in the end Dan-Katsina went down the well and tied the stolen goods to a rope which Dan-Kano let down to him. Dan-Kano thereupon hauled the goods to the top, carried them a little way off from the well and stacked them. Each time he came back to the well, he took a large stone with him and piled these up near the head of the well.

When they had been working like this for some time, Dan-Kano called down the well to his companion. 'Dan-Katsina,' he said, 'when the stuff is all up, and you are ready to come up yourself, give a shout, and I'll haul you up very carefully so that you don't bump yourself against the sides.'

'Very well,' said Dan-Katsina.

They worked away like this until the last bale but one had gone up. But Dan-Katsina was too wily to let Dan-Kano know this, as he had a pretty shrewd idea of what Dan-Kano intended towards him. Instead, he shouted up, 'The next load will be a pretty heavy one, but it is the last.' He then crawled into the last of the bales and hid himself inside.

Dan-Kano now hauled up this last bale and carried it over to where he had stacked the others, not realizing that Dan-Katsina was hidden inside. Then he went back to where he

—'Dan-Katsina crept out of the bale where he had been hiding and started putting all the bales in a different place.'

had collected the pile of stones and started hurling them down into the well where he thought his companion still was.

While Dan-Kano was busy throwing all these stones down the well, Dan-Katsina crept out of the bale where he had been hiding, and started putting all the bales in a different place, behind some bushes. Accordingly, when Dan-Kano came back, he found that all the loot had vanished.

'Well, blow me down!' he exclaimed to himself. 'While I was finishing off Dan-Katsina, someone else must have come along and taken the stuff away.'

It then occurred to Dan-Kano that as the thief could not be far away and would in all probability be needing a pack-animal to carry all the loot, he might well come hurrying back if he heard a donkey braying. No sooner did this idea come to Dan-Kano that he hid in a thicket nearby where he started to bray like a donkey. Sure enough, Dan-Katsina came hurrying up calling out, 'Steady, Neddy! Hold hard there! Come on boy!' When they saw one another, they were speechless for a moment, then Dan-Kano said, 'Dan-Katsina, you're a scoundrel!' to which Dan-Katsina replied, 'And you're another!'

The two rogues collected their booty and took it to Dan-Kano's house. When they got there, Dan-Katsina said, 'I want to go on and visit my family, Dan-Kano, so we'll leave the stuff here and I'll come back in three months' time and we can divide it then.'

'Very well,' said Dan-Kano.

When Dan-Katsina had been gone for two months, Dan-Kano had a grave dug in his compound which he covered over with potsherds and broken calabashes. When the three months were nearly up, he retired into this grave and his family heaped earth over the potsherds and calabashes.

A few days later Dan-Katsina turned up and asked Dan-Kano's family where he was.

'Alas! haven't you heard?' they said. 'Dan-Kano is dead. We buried him four days ago.'

'Really?' said Dan-Katsina. 'Well then, take me to his grave so that I can see it for myself.'

When he was taken to the grave Dan-Katsina broke into loud lamentations. 'So Dan-Kano has gone the way of all flesh!'

A rich man's house in Kano, Northern Nigeria, with geometrical designs moulded in sun-dried mud covered over with cement.

he wept. 'God's will be done. But you know,' he said, addressing Dan-Kano's family, 'you ought to cut thorn-bushes and cover the grave well, otherwise hyenas may come and dig him up and scatter his bones.'

'We'll do it tomorrow,' promised Dan-Kano's relations.

'Now take me to my room,' said Dan-Katsina, 'for tomorrow I must go home.'

In the middle of the night, when every one was asleep, Dan-Katsina got up and crept out of the house and went to Dan-Kano's grave. There he started to growl ferociously – 'Gr, Grrr, Grrrr' – and went on hands and knees and scrabbled at the earth which covered the grave as if he were a hyena trying to get at the corpse within.

Inside the grave Dan-Kano heard this awful noise and scrabbling and was terrified. 'Help, help!' he cried, 'Save me! I'm going to be eaten by a hyena! Let me out of here!'

'All right,' said Dan-Katsina. 'Out you come.'

And so in the end these two rogues, Dan-Kano and Dan-Katsina, had to make a fair and equal division of the goods which they had stolen from the traders.

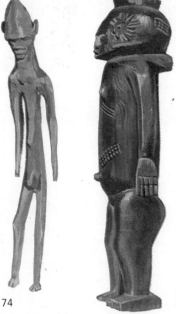

These human figures, from the Bari (l) and the Sobat area (r) typify the 'pole-sculpture' characteristic of the Nilotic Sudan.

Opposite: baked clay figurine of a hyena, from the Shilluk tribe.

74

Nilotic tribes

The Nilotic tribes live chiefly in the Nile valley, in the southern Sudan. They show great aloofness and pride in their race and culture, so that they have changed less in the last hundred years than most other African tribes. They are classified as Nilotes, and though 'black', they are negroid rather than Negro. Physically they are tall, averaging seventy inches in height, slender and long-limbed, with clearcut features and thin lips. The men generally go naked, or wear a short cloak; the women wear short aprons.

In culture they are pastoral to such an extent that the Dinka generally fail to grow enough grain for their needs. This obsessive pastoralism results in an almost religious esteem of their cattle. The Dinka have an initiation ceremony in which the father presents his son with a bull, to which the youth attaches himself so strongly that he identifies with it and spends hours in its company. Cattle are therefore not killed except for ceremonies, and the main diet is milk and grain. Except among the Dinka and Nuer, women have no dealing with cattle during their reproductive life, and the men and

boys tend the cattle, as they do throughout South Africa.

The Dinka and Nuer hunt hippopotamus in dug-out canoes – its flesh forms a considerable part of their diet. Their typical weapon is the spear.

Unlike their neighbours in the Upper Congo watershed, human sacrifice is rare and cannibalism unknown.

The Shilluk have a king, whose function is to make rain. This puts him into Frazer's class of 'Divine King.' He lives in great state, is not allowed into battle and has his homestead on an artificial hill. The spirit of Nyakang, the culture-hero of the Shilluk and traditional founder of the tribe, lives in the king. If the king's health should fail or his virility diminish, the king must die, for the cattle will sicken, the crops wither, and the men perish if the king, Nyakang's earthly body, is not fully vigorous. There is a ritual for the slaying of the old king and the installation of the new one with a transference of Nyakang's spirit.

The man and the snake
(Nuer tribe, Nilotic Sudan)

A man once found some snakes fighting. As he came near and looked at them he saw that one snake had been killed. He reproved them and said, 'Go away.'

One snake gave him a charm, saying, 'By means of this charm you will hear all things. When the rat talks, you will hear it. When the cow talks, you will hear it. You will hear everything.' The man went on his way and came to the village.

At night the man's wife closed the house so that there was no crack left open. All was quite dark. She and her husband lay down to sleep. A mosquito came to the door. It went all over the house and found no way in. The mosquito said, 'They have closed the house very securely. How can one get in?'

The man understood and laughed.

'What are you laughing about?' asked his wife.

'Nothing,' he said.

Later, a rat came. He examined the door. He found it fast closed and left it. Then he tried the eaves of the house and got in. He searched everywhere, looking for butter, but he could find none. He said, 'Oh, where has that woman stored her butter?' The man laughed.

The Nuer way of life revolves around their cattle. These may be milked, but are never killed except for ritual purposes.

His wife asked him, 'What are you laughing about?'

He answered, 'Nothing.'

In the morning the man went to his cattle-pen. He let the cattle out. When it was nearly milking-time his wife came to milk. When she arrived the cow said, 'Of course you come, but you will not milk me today. I shall hold back my milk, and my calf will drink it afterwards.' The man laughed.

His wife asked him, 'What are you laughing at?'

He answered, 'Nothing.'

The wife left the cow and returned to the village without milk. Then the calf sucked its mother.

The next day the wife again came to milk. The cow again withheld its milk. In the afternoon the woman's child was ill for want of milk. She brought it to the cattle-pen and said to her husband, 'That calf will kill my daughter.'

The cow interrupted, 'What! My daughter will kill your daughter?'

The man laughed.

His wife asked him, 'What are you laughing about?'

He answered, 'Nothing.'

At sunset his wife said, 'I shall get a divorce.'

She called all the people. They came to her husband's place. They all sat down. They said to the wife:

'You and your husband talk. We will listen.'

The wife talked. She said to the people, 'When we lie down to sleep, my husband always laughs at me without any reason. When I ask him why he does it he hides the reason from me. That is why I object to him.'

The people then asked the husband, 'Why do you laugh at your wife? Tell us.'

He answered, 'Nothing.'

They said again, 'Tell us.'

He answered, 'Men, if I tell it, I will die.'

They said, 'Tell it, man! Do not hide it.'

He replied, 'Oh, men, I will not tell it. I will surely die if I do.'

They went on asking. When he was worn out he

A Shilluk man with tribal cicatrices on his forehead, and a shock of hair straightened and bleached orange with cattle urine.

In addition to spears and shields and clubs, Nilotic weapons include throwing-knives such as these from the Ingassana and Shilluk.

told them, 'This is the reason why I laughed when we were lying down in the house. After a while at night the mosquito would talk. It would say, "Who is this woman that has locked up her house so tightly? Where can one get in?" That is why I laughed.'

The man died, as he had said. The people mourned. Some of them dug a grave. As they were about to bury the body a snake hurried to the burial place. It wrapped itself round the body and stuck its tail in the nose of the dead man. He sneezed. The people were amazed, and some asked, 'Is it his god?'

Others replied, 'Why ask who it is?'

When the man stood up the snake left.

When the man had quite recovered he travelled through the desolate places. He found the snake under a tree. The snake said, 'But why did you tell? Long ago when I gave you that charm I told you it would make you hear all things.'

The man replied, 'They urged me, so I told them.'

The snake said, 'Oh!'

Then the snake gave him another charm, saying, 'You will hear the words of the birds which eat the kaffir corn. When a bird is in the kaffir corn in the field you will hear its words.'

The snake went away.

The man returned to the village. He heard many things. When a bird was eating the kaffir corn, if another bird came near, the first one would say, 'Bird! Do not come. We shall be seen. I am eating quietly. This is my place. Let us separate. The field is large.'

After a while another bird would reply, 'What!! I shall be found out?' A third would interrupt, 'How will you get out? Perhaps they will find us.'

'Let him go,' cried one bird.

'I am not going,' said the other. The man laughed there in the kaffir corn.

The man always held the snake sacred as his god.

Many Nilotic tribes live in the swampy areas of the Bahr-el-Ghazal, and find dugout canoes a necessity.

Left: Congo influence is shown in the bodily scarification and carving technique of these figures from the Jiji tribe, Tanzania.

Opposite: throne, collected from the palace at Buruku in 1898, belonging to a chief of the Nyamwezi tribe, Tanzania.

Tribes of the East African Hinterland

East Africa is a melting-pot of African races, and also the cradle of man in Africa, as Leakey's excavations have shown. The inhabitants of this area, which comprises Kenya, Uganda, Rwanda, Burundi, Tanzania, Malawi and northern Mozambique, are classified as Negro-Hamitic in varying degree. Hamite invaders became progressively diluted with Negro (Bantu) blood. The Hamites are pre-eminently pastoral, deeply attached to their cattle, and in appearance negroid rather than Negro, tall and slender, with fine 'European' faces, but with negroid hair. The Negroes, whether Sudanese (West Africa) or Bantu (Central, Eastern and Southern Africa) are classified on linguistic grounds.

The people of East Africa are divided into Nilotes, Nilo-Hamites and Bantu.

The Nilo-Hamites are limited to East Africa; the principal tribes include the Masai, Suk and Karamojong. Typically this group consists of nomadic herdsmen, but some tribes are sedentary, combining agriculture and pastoralism. The majority are semi-nomadic but they are becoming more settled in their way of life while retaining their primary interest in cattle-raising. Cattle are sacred to some of these tribes, which may even have separate words for anything at all relevant to cattle, and the Nandi even take care not to mix meat and milk in the stomach by eating both at the same meal. The Masai are usually considered the aristocrats of this group of tribes; they are a handsome people, proud, and still retain much of their original way of life. The men of these tribes generally wear very little clothing, the women wear long leather garments and coiled brass wire ornaments on legs, arms and neck.

The men are circumcised and initiated in age-groups and eventually become warriors. The Masai warrior is expected to kill a lion single-handed with his spear to show his courage.

When about thirty, they retire, marry and become elders. Cattle are the main form of wealth, necessary in the buying of a wife. Among some tribes, blood, drawn from a vein in the cow's neck, is a favourite food for the men.

In religion all the tribes of this area believe in a Supreme Being, but the cult of ancestors as mediators may be important too. The medicine man is also important; he practises divination to foretell the future, makes rain, causes fertility, advises when to plant crops, and will decide if the omens are favourable for war.

The Interlacustrine Bantu live around the Great Lakes. In this group come the powerful tribal kingdoms of Buganda, Bunyoro and Bunyankole. Here, typically among the Batutsi, sometimes one may find a cattle-owning Hamiticised aristocracy, characteristically slender, two metres tall, among a Negro peasant or serf population, shorter, with coarser features, and plainly a different race. Kintu, the traditional founder of these tribes, came from the north with one each of cow, chicken, banana root and sweet potato, which miraculously increased and stocked the country. The administrative detail of Buganda is highly organised.

In material culture this group of tribes is perhaps the most advanced of East Africa. Hut architecture is particularly good; the royal huts and enclosures are even palatial, embellished with patterned mats of plaited elephant grass. In the King's compound there is an enclosure for the sacred royal drums, which receive offerings of beer and milk. When a king died, his wives and retainers were sacrificed.

The Akamba and Kikuyu are probably the most important tribes of the Eastern Bantu. They are primarily agriculturalists, culturally influenced by the Masai, and like them, frequently bleeding their cattle. The blood is drunk or made into soup.

The Makonde, possibly under early Baluba influence, are the chief sculpture-producing tribe in East Africa. Such sculpture as is found in this area tends to show influence from the Congo, and occurs mainly among the Bantu tribes. Hamitic influence, with the consequent nomadic, pastoral life, probably explains why there is so much less sculpture, pottery and material culture in East Africa than in West Africa and the Congo.

Opposite: this wooden slit gong, 7½ feet long, from the Yangere tribe, is in the form of a bush cow.

Right: this articulated wooden grave figure from the Wasaramo tribe of Tanzania seems to have been made to be seated.

Iron sculptures such as this bull are rare in African art. These two were discovered by the Stanley Expedition in 1876.

How Walukaga the blacksmith answered the King
(Baganda Tribe, Uganda, East Africa)

There was once, a long time ago, a blacksmith named Walukaga, who was a skilful blacksmith, the most skilful in the whole country. He was the chief of the king's blacksmiths, and he would make all sorts of things – hoes for the farmers and women, knives and spears for the men and warriors, bill-hooks and axes to cut back the forest; and as well as that he was able to make wonderful figures of iron for the king.

One day a messenger came to summon Walukaga to the king's house, saying that the king had a special task for him. Walukaga obeyed this summons gladly and, after putting on his best toga of patterned barkcloth, he went to the king, and was soon received into the inner courtyard where the king sat in audience. Walukaga went up to the king and made obeisance, touching his forehead to the ground. The king then said, 'Walukaga, you are the chief of my blacksmiths and the most skilful. None other of my smiths can make iron figures to equal the ones you have made. But now I have a great task for you, that only you can possibly carry out.'

So saying, he clapped his hands, and some attendants came in bringing a great quantity of iron all ready for working. The king continued: 'Walukaga, I want you to take this iron and forge it and hammer it and make a man for me. I do not want a small statue and I do not want an ancestor-statue. I want a real man, man-size in iron, who can walk and talk, who has blood in his veins, knowledge in his head, and feelings in his heart.'

This female antelope, together with the bull and two similar figures, came from the palace of Chief Rumanika in Karagwe.

Walukaga heard the king's words with amazement and despair, but he touched his forehead to the ground again and took the iron home without protest. He knew how absolute the king's power and the king's wishes were, and that if he could not do as the king commanded, he and all his family would have to die by drinking from the poison pot. From that moment he had no peace of mind. He racked his brains, but he could not think how to begin. He visited all his fellow-smiths and all his friends and told them of his problem and implored them to help him and think of something. Alas, not one of them could advise him.

Of course, there were impractical suggestions. He could try making an iron shell of a man and find someone to get inside it to make it speak and move. But this would not be an honest attempt that would satisfy the king. Or he could just leave the country and go somewhere, many days' journey distant, beyond the king's power and where no one had heard of him, and start a new life there, since a good blacksmith is never short of work. But this would mean leaving friends and relations behind him, who might suffer from the king's anger.

Walukaga was walking home through the bush one day, after visiting some friends and asking their advice. On his way he met a friend who had gone mad and was now living out in the wild, quite alone. Walukaga had not heard that this friend had gone mad, but when he greeted him the madman recognized him, and answered quite rationally. So they both sat down together and talked of this and that, and then the madman asked Walukaga what he was doing now. To this Walukaga, sighing deeply, answered that he was in great trouble and despair and in danger of death. The madman was sympathetic and asked for the story. Walukaga, reflecting that his friend seemed rational enough at the moment and that telling his story could do no harm, told all the tale of the king's impossible command and his difficulty in carrying it out. The madman listened quietly to the very end, and when Walukaga, half seriously, asked what he should do, burst out into hearty laughter.

Then he said, 'If the king asks you for the impossible, you must do no less. Go then to the king, and tell him that if he really wishes you to make this wonderful man forged out of cold iron, that can walk and talk, with blood in his veins, knowledge in his head, and feelings in his heart, it is essential for you to have, as well as the iron, special charcoal for the fire and special water to slake the fire and keep it from burning too fiercely. Tell him, then, to order all the people of the kingdom to shave their heads and burn the hair until they have made one thousand loads of charcoal, and that they must weep until there are one hundred pots full of water from their eyes.'

Walukaga was most grateful for this advice, which was by far the best he had had, and he lost no time in going to the king's house, where he asked for an audience.

When Walukaga was admitted to the king's presence, he bowed low, and then said, 'Master, if you really want me to make this wonderful iron man in the manner you have described, I must have special fuel and special water to slake the fire.' The king was so anxious to

Figure of Gu, god of war, over five feet high, made by the Fon of Dahomey, probably out of ship's iron.

Tribes such as the Baganda of Uganda show real artistry in making these plumbago-burnished pots in the form of gourds.

Prisoners condemned to death had to drink poisoned beer from special three-spouted pots like this one from the Baganda.

have the iron man that he readily agreed to give him whatever he needed. So Walukaga went on: 'Master, you must order all the people to shave their heads and burn their hair to make one thousand loads of charcoal for me to heat the iron. Further, you must have them collect one hundred water-pots full of tears to act as water to slake the fire and keep it from burning too fiercely. Ordinary charcoal from wood, and the ordinary water from wells are of no use for forging an iron man.'

Accordingly, the king sent messages to all parts of the kingdom commanding his people, that all of them should shave their heads for charcoal and shed their tears for water.

All his subjects tried their best as they were afraid of

the king's power, but when all of them had done their utmost, and all heads were smooth-shaven and all eyes were squeezed dry of tears, there was not even one load of charcoal and not even two water-pots full of tears.

The elders of the kingdom came and told this to the king. He pondered the matter for a bit and then sent for Walukaga, who, guessing what was afoot came to the king's house in some trepidation. However, when he looked up after making obeisance, the king said, 'Walukaga, do not try any more to make the iron man for me. I am unable to give you the charcoal and the water that you asked for.'

Walukaga again touched his forehead to the ground and thanked the king. Then he looked up and said, 'Master, it was because I knew that you would never be able to get enough hair for the charcoal and enough tears for the water that I asked for them; you had asked me to do an impossible thing when you commanded me to forge a real man, who could walk and talk, with blood in his veins, knowledge in his head and feeling in his heart.'

All the king's people that were there laughed and said, 'Walukaga speaks the truth.'

The girl who was sacrificed by her family and whom her lover brought back from below
(Kikuyu tribe, Kenya, East Africa)

The sun was very hot and there was no rain, so the crops died and everyone was very hungry. Things happened this way one year, and again for a second year, and even a third year, that the rains did not come and the crops failed. The people all assembled on the great open space on the hilltop, where they usually met to dance, and they said to each other, 'Why do the rains not come?' They went to the witch-doctor, and they said to him, 'Tell us why there is no rain for even a third season, for our crops have withered and we shall die of hunger.'

The witch-doctor took his gourd and shook it, and poured its contents on to the ground. He did this many times, and at last he said, 'There is a maiden called Wanjiru. If rain is to fall she must be bought by the people. The day after tomorrow you must all return to this place, and every one

— 'He was received into the inner courtyard where the King sat in audience . . . the King's power and wishes were absolute.'

Clay fertility figures of a man and woman, made and used by the Kikuyu of Kenya during harvest-time dances.

of you from the eldest to the youngest must bring with him a goat for the purchase of this maiden.'

On the appointed day, old men and young men were all gathered together, each one leading a goat. Now they all stood in a circle, with Wanjiru in the middle, and her relations in a group to one side. As they stood there, and people began to bring goats in payment, the feet of Wanjiru began to sink into the ground, and she sank in up to her knees and cried out in terror, 'I am lost!'

Her father and mother saw what was happening, and they, too, cried out in terror.

The people saw this wonder, and they crowded forward and gave goats to Wanjiru's father and mother. Wanjiru sank lower, up to her waist, and again she cried out, 'I am lost, but much rain will come!'

She sank to her breast, but the rain did not come, though there were heavy black clouds in the sky. Wanjiru said again, 'Much rain will come.'

Now she sank in up to her neck, and the rain began to fall in great drops. Her family would now have rushed forward to save her, but yet more people came, pressing them to take goats in payment, so they stayed still.

Then Wanjiru wailed, 'My people have forsaken me!' and she sank down yet lower. As one after another of her family stepped forward to save her, someone in the crowd would give him a goat, and he would retire. And Wanjiru lamented for the last time, a great cry, 'I am undone, and my people have forsaken me!' Then she disappeared, the earth closed over her, and the rain poured down in a heavy torrent, and all the people hurried back home.

Now there was a young warrior who loved Wanjiru, and he mourned continually, saying, 'Wanjiru is lost, and her own people have done this thing.' And he said, 'Where has Wanjiru gone? I will go to the same place.' So he took his shield and spear, and he wandered over the country day and night until one evening, as dusk fell, he came to the spot where Wanjiru had vanished. Then he stood where she had stood, and as he stood, his feet began to sink as hers had sunk;

—'Wanjiru sank lower, up to her waist, and again she cried, "I am lost, but much rain will come!"'

and he sank lower and lower until the ground closed over him, and he went by a long road under the earth, following Wanjiru, and at length he saw her. But indeed, she was in a pitiable state, tired and cold and hungry, and her clothing had rotted away. He said to her, 'You were sacrificed to bring the rain; now the rain has come, and I shall bring you back.' So he carried Wanjiru on his back as if she had been a child and brought her to the road he had come by, and they rose together to the open air, and their feet stood once more on the ground above.

Then the warrior said, 'You shall not return to the house of your people, for they have treated you shamefully.' And

This young Kikuyu is standing at ease in an attitude typical of the Nilotes and related peoples of East Africa.

When dancing, young Kikuyu men wear these shields on the upper left arm, causing them to vibrate like butterflies' wings.

he told her to wait till nightfall. When it was dark he took her to the house of his mother and he asked his mother to leave, saying that he had private business.

But his mother said, 'Why do you hide this thing from me, seeing that I am your mother who bore you?' So he told his mother, but cautioned her, 'Tell no one that Wanjiru has come back.'

So Wanjiru stayed in his mother's house. He and his mother killed goats, and she ate and grew strong. Then they made clothes for her out of the skins, so that she was most beautifully dressed.

The next day there was a great dance, and her lover went with everyone else. But his mother and the girl waited till everyone was there and then they came out of the house and joined the crowd. When the relations saw Wanjiru, they said, 'Surely that is Wanjiru whom we had lost.'

And they wanted to greet her, but her lover beat them off, for he said, 'You sold Wanjiru shamefully.'

Then she returned to his mother's house. But the next day her family again came, and the warrior relented, for he said, 'Surely they are her father and her mother and her brothers.'

So he paid them the bride-price, and he married Wanjiru who had been lost.

97

The Pare of Tanzania make clay figures like this, to put in the hut yard to drive away thieves and enemies.

A rich man and a poor man
(Akamba tribe, Kenya, East Africa)

Long, long ago, in one of the villages of the Akamba, there were two men who lived as neighbours. One was rich, and the other was poor, but in spite of that they were good friends. The poor man worked for the rich man, helping him. Now it so happened that there was a famine in the land, and the crops failed and the cattle grew thin. When the hunger became very great the rich man grew hard-hearted towards the poor man, and he who used to eat at his rich friend's house now went begging for some food. Indeed, the rich man chased him away from the village, because a well-to-do man cannot be friendly with a poor person for too long, and also he did feel that his poor neighbour was eating too much of his food.

Well, one day this poor man was looking for something to

eat, and another man who took pity on him gave him some maize. The poor man took the maize back to his hut, gave it to his wife, and she cooked a maize-meal. But they had no meat with which to prepare a gravy-stew, and they did not even have any salt to season it. So the poor man said, 'I will go and see if my rich friend is having a savoury meal prepared for him.' He went to the rich man's house and found that this was indeed the case, and the aroma appetizing. So he returned to his hut, took the maize-meal and sat against the wall of the rich man's house and ate his food while breathing in the smell that came from this rich dinner cooking. After he had eaten, he returned home.

A few days later, the poor man met the rich man and told him, 'A few days ago I came while your food was being cooked, and I sat by the wall and ate my maize-meal together with the delicious smell that came from your food.' At this the rich

Akamba elders use these distinctive stools with hammered-in patterns made in spirally-wound brass, copper or aluminium wire.

man was furious and he shouted, 'So that is why my food was quite tasteless that day. If it was you who ate the good taste from my food you must pay me for it. I will take you to the judge and file a case against you.'

So they went to the judge, and the poor man was told to pay one goat to the rich man as indemnity for eating the taste from his food. But the poor man could not afford even one goat, and he broke down and cried as he went back to his hut.

On his way home he met a friend who was a lawyer, and he told him what had happened. The lawyer gave the poor man a goat, and told him to keep that goat safely till the appointed day . Now the judge had named a certain day when the poor man had to make payment, and on that day a crowd of people assembled to watch. The lawyer came also, and when he saw this crowd he asked, 'What's happening here?' The judge explained, 'This poor man is supposed to pay this rich man a goat as payment for the sweet smell he breathed from the rich man's food.' The lawyer could hardly believe his ears and asked his question again and received the same answer. So then the lawyer said, 'Will you let me give another opinion?' The people said, 'Yes, if you are a good judge!' So he continued, 'If this poor man ate or breathed only the smell, then he must pay that smell back and nothing more. The smell was savoured by every other person and animal in the house. But if the poor man ate food, then he should be made to pay back that food.'

The people asked him, 'How can the poor man pay back the smell of good food?' The lawyer said, 'I will show you!' Then turning to the rich man, he continued, 'I am going to beat this goat, and when it bleats you must take the sound of its bleating! But you may not take this poor man's goat unless he took your food.' So he beat the goat, and it bleated, and he said to the rich man, 'Take that sound as payment for the smell of your good food!' Everybody clapped their hands with great joy, and accepted the verdict then and there. They all went home, and the lawyer reclaimed his goat. So the poor man was saved from the oppression of the rich man.

—'So he beat the goat, and it bleated, and he said to the rich man, "Take that sound as payment!"'

This stool from the Congo Baluba, about ten inches high, gains monumental stability from the elephant's flaring legs.

The hare and the elephant
(Akamba tribe, Kenya, East Africa)

One day the hare said to the elephant, 'Let's meet in the big forest over there, so that we can have a race and see who runs the faster.' The elephant agreed to this. Then the hare went to his wife and said, 'Tomorrow you must be at the great tree in the forest, and when the elephant arrives you must say to him, "I reached the tree a long time ago. This is the finishing place!" '

The following morning, the hare and the elephant went to the edge of the big forest and started running. The elephant pushed his way through the trees and the thick undergrowth but the hare just hopped here and there. After a while he went back to the starting-place and hid himself.

Meanwhile the elephant had reached the great tree, and there he found the hare's wife resting and waiting for him. She greeted him, 'Oh my friend! I arrived here a long time ago. I have beaten you.' The elephant answered, 'Never mind. Let us now run back to where we started.'

Off they went again, but the hare's wife hid in the undergrowth while the elephant was struggling on. When he arrived back at the starting-point, there was the hare waiting for him. He said, 'I have beaten you again, my friend.'

The elephant was disappointed at losing the race a second time and said, 'Why can't I run as fast as you do?' The hare replied, 'Maybe it is on account of your fat buttocks.' At that the elephant asked the hare to cut them off so that he could run really fast.

After this operation, the elephant challenged the hare to one more race. They ran, and this time the elephant beat the hare, because the hare had not told his wife to wait at the finishing-point. This convinced the elephant who said, 'I believe you, my friend, that my big bottom kept me from running fast.'

But the elephant's wound did not heal; on the contrary, it got worse. So the elephant called the leopard and said to him, 'Go to the hare and tell him that I want to have my buttocks put back.' The leopard went to the hare's house, found him sitting outside and delivered the message. The hare said, 'The food is nearly ready; stay and eat with us, and after we have fed you can go back to the elephant.' The leopard agreed willingly and ate a good meal. Then the hare told him that the meat they had eaten was the elephant's buttocks. So the leopard thought better about returning to the elephant, who has remained without buttocks to this day.

The Mwera tribe of Tanzania carved this hare mask, with its elongated ears and human-looking bearded face.

The serene expression and harmoniously curving bovine horns make this Baluba mask a beautiful example of Congolese carving.

Bantu tribes of Central Africa

These tribes, otherwise classified as the Western Bantu, are included in the political areas of Angola, all the Congolese countries, Cameroon, the Central African Republic, and Zambia. This vast area is the true 'Heart of Africa,' the tropical rain forest of the Congo, which included the territory of such considerable kingdoms as the mediaeval empires of Kongo and Lunda, and later the Bakuba empire. There are over 150 tribes in this area speaking different Bantu or semi-Bantu languages.

Diogo Cão, who discovered the Congo in 1484 at the instance of Prince Henry the Navigator, found that the chiefs, from the Congo to the Kwilu and Cuanza rivers, were under one king, the King of Kongo, who maintained great state. Portuguese needs for slaves in Brazil soon led to the abandonment of Portuguese hopes of creating a Christian state in Africa, and in the eighteenth century the kingdom lost all

The concept of vital force is thought to be embodied in this *kifwebe* mask from the Basonge.

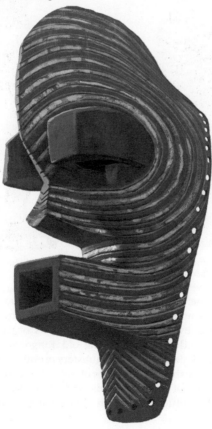

The crude vigour of the Basonge fetish (l) opposes the sensitivity of form and decoration in the Bena Lulua figure (r).

its power. Other powerful kingdoms were the Lunda, Kasongo and Bakuba empires. The Bakuba empire was still powerful when studied by Torday in 1907-8 and its organization to some extent reflected that of the old Kingdom of Kongo. There was a whole hierarchy of ministers presided over by the king, and below them were grades of numerous court officials, representatives of trades, guilds and subtribes (including pygmies). The official historian was an important person, who had to be a king's son, and was responsible for preserving ancient legend and history. The king was of semi-divine status, with a lineage traced back through 120 predecessors, of which the earlier ones are probably mythical. The ninety-third king on the list, Shamba Bolongongo, reigned 1600-1620 (?), and is the national hero, who really seems to have been a remarkable person. He reorganized the government, encouraged arts and crafts, and tried to abolish war by forbidding the *shongo* (throwing-knife) and bow. In his reign the use of tobacco, palm oil, cassava, and raffia weaving and embroidery began, also the unique series of royal portraits.

Congo art is outstanding for its richness of surface texture, whether in treatment of cicatrizations on human or sculptured bodies, or interlacing patterns on wooden vessels, basketry and raffia cloths, but at the same time there is masterly handling of mass and line.

The Bakongo fetish figures (l) are fairly recent; their soapstone ancestor figures (r) much older. This is about 250 years old.

How the dog came to live with man

(Bushongo Tribe, Congo)

A long, long time ago, soon after the beginning of things, the dog and the jackal were brothers, and they lived together in the wilderness. They hunted together and shared their food when it was plentiful and suffered hunger together when it was scarce, and when night came they would curl up together and keep warm in the same shelter.

One day it so happened that they had very bad luck in hunting, even though they had worked hard at it all day and searched everywhere for game. When night came they had had nothing to eat and they felt miserably hungry and tired. What was even worse, it was a very cold night, and already they were shivering. Their shelter of leaves in a hollow was not enough to keep the wind out.

'Bulu,' said the dog after a while.

'Yes?' answered the jackal.

'It is a very bad thing to be tired after hunting all day as we have done, and it is even worse to be ravenously hungry and cold as well,' said the dog.

'Very true,' said the jackal, 'but talking about it won't make things any better. Let us curl up together and try to sleep now. It will make us forget our hunger and tomorrow we may find food.'

So they both curled up and tried to sleep. After a while the dog spoke again.

– 'Bulu.'

– 'Mmm?'

– 'Man has a village near here.'

– 'True. But what has that got to do with us?'

– 'There is a good fire burning inside the man's hut,' the dog explained. 'Maybe if we could creep near that fire we could get some warmth.'

– 'Maybe.'

– 'One might even find some bones and scraps that Man had thrown aside by that fire. The bones might fill our emptiness.'

'Stop talking nonsense and go to sleep,' advised the jackal. 'Thinking about that fire and those bones will only make you suffer the more from hunger and cold.' And he covered his

The Bakuba (Bushongo) show great artistry in their carved wooden boxes and cups, and their raffia velvet pile cloth.

Dogs are hardly represented in African art unless in this type of fetish from the Bakongo. Each nail represents an offering.

Opposite: an idealized portrait of King Kata Mbula, 109th King of the Bakuba (1800–1810). Seventeen similar royal portraits survive.

face with his tail again and dozed off.

The dog tried to follow the jackal's example, but without success. So he persisted. 'Why don't we go and see if we can lie down by that fire?'

'Not I,' said the jackal firmly, opening one eye. 'He who gives advice should be the first to follow it. If you are suffering from cold and hunger as badly as all that, just you be the one to go and look for that fire and that bone.'

'I'm afraid to go near Man all by myself,' whimpered the dog, who really was cold to the bone. He curled up even closer to the jackal and tried his utmost to go to sleep. But it was impossible: the dog's fur was less thick than the jackal's, and because of this he felt the cold more acutely.

At last the dog could bear it no longer. He jumped up and said, 'I'm almost dead of cold and hunger. Nothing could be worse than this, so whatever you do, I am going to see if I can get near that fire. You can stay here if you like, but if I am away too long you'd better come and look for me.'

'Very good,' said the jackal.

Then the dog started trotting towards the village. As he got nearer he went more and more slowly and cautiously so as to remain unobserved, but even so the man's fowls, which were roosting in a tree close to the hut, heard him and started to cackle loudly. At once the man came running

Shamba Bolongongo (1600–1620), King of the Bakuba, reputedly initiated the weaving and embroidery of this type of raffia cloth.

out of the hut with his spear all ready to throw. He saw the dog, who in those days was considered to be a wild animal, and a poacher of fowls, and was going to kill him, when the dog cried out, 'Do not kill me, I beg you. I am only a poor creature dying of hunger and I am already half dead of cold. Please let me warm myself a little by the fire and then I will go back into the bush.'

The man looked at the dog and saw that he was indeed in a pitiable state, shivering and shaking with cold. So he said, 'All right then. Since it is such a cold night you may come inside and warm yourself, but when you are warm, psst! Back you go into the thickets.' The dog crawled into the hut, and lay down thankfully by the fire. After a while he stopped shivering, and then he saw a bone which the man had thrown to the ground. He started to gnaw it, and soon he was feeling much better.

But after a while the man, who was not anxious to have this wild animal staying too long in his hut, asked, 'Are you warm enough to go out now?'

The dog answered, 'Not yet,' for he had just seen another bone.

A little later the man asked again, 'Well, are you warm enough to go now?'

Again the dog answered, 'Not yet,' for he had not quite finished with the bone. The fire was warm and comforting and the bones filled the dog's emptiness. He was most un-willing to go back to the darkness and coldness outside.

The man asked for a third time, 'Are you warm enough to go now?' and now he sounded impatient. The dog was so

Anthropomorphic cup, showing an elaborately cicatrized torso. Such cups were used for ceremonial palm-wine drinking. Bakuba.

A wooden disk, rubbed along this animal's back, would stick when the Bakuba diviner suggested the correct answer to his question.

comfortable that by now he had made up his mind to stay with the man if at all possible.

So he looked up at the man and answered, 'Frankly, yes, but I wish that you would let me stay with you. I would not steal your poultry like my brother the jackal does, indeed, I would keep watch at night and warn you of any danger. I can catch rats, and could keep them from stealing the corn in your granaries. I could help you to hunt the birds of the forest; when you shoot them I will bring their bodies back to you. When you hunt wild animals I could teach you their tricks and use my nose to follow their trail, and when they are wounded I will help to pull them down. All that I ask for in return is a place near your fire and what is left over from your food.'

The man looked carefully into the dog's eyes and decided that he was speaking sincerely. 'Let it be so,' he said, and since that day the dog has lived with man. He guards the man's house and livestock and other property and warns him of any intruders, he helps man with his hunting and wears a wooden bell round his neck so that the man may follow him through the forest as he tracks down game. In return he has a place by Man's fire and eats the remains of his food.

But at night, the jackal, who is now lonely, comes near the village and calls to the dog, who was his brother, to leave Man and come back to the wilderness. So if you hear a plaintive 'Bo-ah' in the night, you may be sure that it is the jackal calling to his brother the dog, who will be sitting in his place by Man's fire.

Why there are cracks in Tortoise's shell
(Ba-Ila tribe, Zambia)

Mr Tortoise, who was married to Mrs Tortoise, had in Vulture a friend who was always visiting him. But, as he had no wings, Tortoise was unable to return the visits, and this upset him. One day, he was thinking and said to his wife, 'Wife!'

Mrs Tortoise answered, 'Hello, husband. What is it?'

He said, 'Don't you see, wife, that we are becoming despicable in Vulture's eyes?'

'How so?'

'Despicable, because it is despicable and unfriendly for me not to visit Vulture. He is always coming here and I have never yet been to his house to visit him – and he is my friend.'

Mrs Tortoise replied, 'I don't see how Vulture could think badly of us unless we could fly as he does and yet did not pay him a visit.'

But Mr Tortoise persisted, 'Nevertheless wife, it is despicable.'

His wife said, 'Very well, then, the only solution is for you to

A large basket, sewn in concentric coils, ornamented with geometric patterns and animals, from Barotseland in Zambia.

These headrests, typical of the Mashona-Makalanga tribes, can show a great variety of geometric designs within the type.

sprout some wings and fly and visit your friend Vulture.'

Mr Tortoise answered, 'No, I shan't sprout any wings because I was not born that way.'

'Well,' said Mrs Tortoise, 'what will you do?'

'I shall find a way,' he replied.

'Find it then,' said Mrs Tortoise, 'and let us see what you will do.'

Later on, Tortoise said to his wife, 'Come and tie me up in a parcel with a lump of tobacco and, when Vulture arrives give it to him and say that it is tobacco to buy grain for us.' So Mrs Tortoise took some palm leaf and made him into a parcel together with a lump of tobacco and put him down in the corner.

At his usual time Vulture came to pay his visit, and said, 'Where's your husband gone, Mrs Tortoise?'

'My husband has gone quite a distance to visit some people, and he left hunger here. We have not a bit of grain in the house.'

Vulture said, 'You are indeed in trouble, if you have not any grain.'

Mrs Tortoise replied, 'We are in such trouble as human

beings never knew.' And she went on, 'Vulture, at your place could one buy any grain to end the hunger?'

'Yes,' said he, 'any amount, Mrs Tortoise.'

She brought the bundle and said, 'My husband left this lump of tobacco thinking you might use it to buy some grain for us and bring it here.'

Vulture took the parcel willingly and returned to his home in the heights. As he was nearing his native town he was surprised to hear a voice saying, 'Untie me, I am your friend Tortoise. I said I would pay a visit to you.'

But Vulture was so surprised that he let go of the parcel and down crashed Tortoise to the earth – *pididi-pididi!* His shell smashed to bits when he hit the earth, and he died. And so the friendship between Tortoise and Vulture was broken: and you can still see the cracks in Tortoise's shell.

These masks are worn by the Mbunda tribe of Barotseland, Zambia, at the *makishi* dances, held at every new moon.

117

Great Zimbabwe may have been a sanctuary or a hill-top fort; these massive walls were built soon after A.D.1500.

Bantu tribes of South-East Africa

This is the region south of the Zambezi and Kunene rivers, and extends over a vast area.

All the Bantu are true Negroes, but with varying admixtures of Hamitic or Bushman or Hottentot blood which causes variation in physical appearance. They are thought to have reached this area about the eleventh century A.D.

In Rhodesia there are dry-stone ruins, some of great size and complexity, the most famous being Zimbabwe. These may be a survival from the Monomotapa Kingdom, discovered by Portuguese explorers, and thought to be Ophir.

The Zulu and Ndebele (Matabele) are perhaps the best known tribes. Some tribes attained great power under strong chiefs, e.g. the Basuto under Moshesh in the nineteenth century, and especially the Zulu who rose to power under Chaka from 1810 onwards until the annexation of Zululand by the British in 1887.

The way of life under all these tribes is broadly similar. They lived in enclosed villages or kraals which might house one or several extended families with all their related kin. Cattle-keeping was important and wealth was reckoned in cattle. Daughters were welcomed, since an aspiring suitor had to pay many cattle as *lobola* or bride-price which in its turn would enable the sons to marry without impoverishing the parents. Then the new wife could swell the labour-force in the fields.

The story chosen here is a profound one, illustrating the retribution that follows if tribal custom and man's place in the universe are not respected. In the story that follows the young man flouts custom by refusing to marry within his own group or to let his parents choose his wife or visit his prospective in-laws and bring the bride-price themselves.

The Makonde of northern Tanzania and southern Mozambique carved this, the best of several figures of dancing women.

The woman is equally non-conformist. She refuses the woman helpers her parents offer, insisting instead on having the Rover of the Plain, the buffalo in whom the tribe has life.

The man has to be punished, but the punishment is subtle in that he is at once the instrument and a victim of the final disaster. Every time the woman revives the buffalo that her husband has shot, the real world that she has outraged intervenes through her husband or her mother-in-law. And so the buffalo dies, and the woman and her tribe must perish.

Masks of this type, with lip-plugs and facial scarifications rendered in applied beeswax, are characteristic of the Makonde.

The Makonde and related tribes are the most accomplished carvers of East Africa; this is one of their most beautiful masks.

The Rover of the Plain
(Baronga Tribe, Mozambique)

Once there were a man and a woman who had two children, a boy and a girl. When the girl was old enough she was married and her husband gave a herd of cattle to the parents as bride-price, for that was the custom. Now the parents said to their son, 'Now we have a herd of cattle and are able to buy you a wife. It is time that you married and we will choose you a pretty girl, of a good family, and able to work well.'

But the son did not want things to be done according to the custom of the tribe. 'No,' he said, 'do not bother. I do not fancy any of the girls of this tribe. If I must marry, let me do things my own way, let me go further afield and choose my wife for myself.'

'Do as you wish,' replied the parents, 'but if you find unhappiness, blame yourself, not us.'

Then the young man left the country of his tribe and travelled far, very far, into unknown places. As last he came to a village where he saw maidens pounding corn, and others cooking. He stood for a while watching them and listening to the thumping of the heavy pestles in the mortars. One of the maidens attracted him, and he said to himself, 'That one there

121

is the one I would like to marry.' Then he went to the village elders and said, 'Good day, Fathers!'

'Good day, young man!' they answered. 'What brings you here?'

'I want to look at your daughters, to choose a wife.'

'Well, well,' they said, 'we will show them to you, and then you can make your choice.'

So they led all their daughters past him, and among them was the maiden that attracted him. So he made his choice, and the girl agreed at once to marry him.

'Your parents, we expect, will visit us, as the custom is and bring the bride-price, will they not?' asked the girl's parents.

'No, not at all,' answered the young man. 'I have the bride-price with me, see, here it is.'

'Then,' they persisted, 'at least they will come later in order to conduct your wife to you, as the custom is?'

'No, no,' said the young man. 'I fear they would only upset you with the strict advice they would give your daughter. Let me, myself, take her along to my people now.'

The maiden's parents had to agree to an immediate marriage, but they took her aside to advise her how to behave. 'Be good and helpful to your parents-in-law and be obedient and take faithful care of your husband!' they said. Then they offered the young bride one of her sisters, as the custom was, to help with work in the house and the fields. But the daughter would not consider any of them, though she was offered two, ten, twenty to choose from, all of them handpicked.

'No, no,' she insisted, 'I do not want them. Give me instead the buffalo of the country, our own buffalo, the Rover of the Plain. Let him be my servant.'

'How can you possibly ask for him?' her parents protested. 'You know that all our lives depend on him. Here he is well looked after, but how will you do that in a strange country where he is unknown? He will starve and die, and then all of us will die with him.'

Before she left her parents to go to her new home, the young wife collected together a bundle of medicinal roots, a cupping

—'At last he came to a village where he saw maidens pounding corn, and . . . stood for a while watching them.'

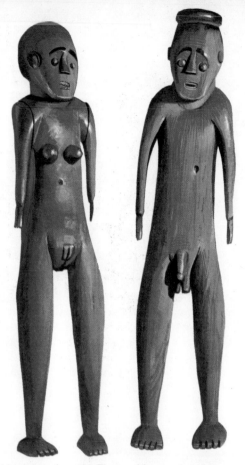

These old carvings from the Thonga-Magwamba tribes are characteristic of the more naive sculpture of Southern Africa.

horn, a little sharp knife, and a gourd full of fat, all of which she took with her in a pot.

Then she set out with her husband. The buffalo followed them, but she alone could see him. The man did not see him. He did not suspect that the Rover of the Plain was the servant accompanying his wife.

As soon as the couple arrived at the husband's village, his

people greeted them joyfully and cried out, 'Hoyo! Hoyo!'

'Now look at him!' said the old parents. 'So you did find a wife after all! You did not want one of those we suggested for you, but that makes no difference. You have done as you wished and chosen your wife for yourself. If, however, you have trouble some time, you will have no right to complain.'

The man then took his wife out into the fields and showed her which ones were his own and which ones belonged to his mother. The young woman noted everything and returned with him to the village. But on the way back she said, 'I have lost my beads and they must be in the field; I want to go back and look for them'. This was an excuse, for she really wanted to see the buffalo and tell him what to do. She told him, 'Here is the boundary of the fields, where I can meet you. Stay here! And over there is the forest where you can hide.'

Now whenever the wife wanted any water, she merely went to the boundary of the fields and put the water-pot down in front of the buffalo. He ran with it to the lake, filled it, and brought it back to his mistress. Whenever she told him that she wanted wood, he would go into the bush, break trees with his horns, and bring her back as much as she needed.

The people in the village knew nothing of this and so they were amazed at her. 'What strength she has!' they said. 'She is always back with the water right away, and she gathers wood in the twinkling of an eye.' But no one suspected that she had a buffalo for a servant.

Wooden food dish from Barotseland, Zambia, with buffalo carved on the lid. Other animals may be shown, especially ducks.

— 'The people in the village . . . were amazed at her. "She is always back with the water right away."'

However, the wife did not bring the buffalo anything to eat, for she had only one dish for herself and her husband. At her parent's home, of course, they had had a separate dish for the Rover of the Plain and fed him with the best food. So here, the buffalo was hungry. Every day the woman would bring him her water-pot and send him to fill it for her. He did this willingly, but he felt great hunger.

One day the woman showed him a corner in the bush and told him to clear it, ready for cultivation. During the night the buffalo took a hoe and prepared a great field. Everyone in the village marvelled at this, saying, 'How skilful she is! And how fast she has done her work!'

That very next evening the buffalo said to his mistress, 'I am hungry, and since I came here I have had nothing to eat. Soon I shall be unable to work any more!'

'Aie!' cried the woman in distress, 'What shall I do? We

126

have only one dish at the house. The people at home were right when they said you would have to start stealing. So then, steal! Go into my field and take a bean here and there. And then, go further afield. But do not take all the food from the same spot, and then the owners may not notice it so much and will be less alarmed.'

That night, accordingly, the buffalo went into the fields. He ate a bean here and a bean there, jumped from one corner to the other, and finally retreated to his hiding-place. When the women came to work in the fields the next morning, they could hardly believe their eyes. 'Hey, hey, what is going on here? A wild beast has destroyed our plants! See, one can even follow his tracks. Ho, the poor land!' So they ran back and told the story in the village.

That evening, the woman said to the buffalo, 'To be sure, they were very much terrified, but not too much, all the same. So you had better steal somewhere else tonight!'. And so it con-

Children of the Sotho tribe made these attractive clay figures of cattle to play with.

tinued. The women who owned the fields made a great to-do and at last they turned to the men and asked them to lie in wait for the raider with their guns.

Now the woman's husband was a very good marksman. So he lay in ambush close by his wife's field and waited. The buffalo, who thought that someone might be lying in wait for him where he had stolen the night before, went this time to his mistress's beans, where he had fed the first time.

'Why!' exclaimed the man, 'this is a buffalo! I have never seen one in this country before. This is indeed a rare animal.' He fired. The bullet pierced the buffalo's head, close to the ear and came out exactly opposite on the other side. The Rover of the Plain leaped into the air and fell dead.

'That was a good shot!' exclaimed the man, and he went back to the village and told them.

But the woman now began to cry out in pain and clutched her belly. 'Oh, I have pains in my stomach, oh! oh!'

'Calm yourself!' they told her. The woman seemed sick, but this was only a pretence, as she had to explain why she was crying thus, and why she seemed so upset when she heard of the buffalo's death. They gave her medicine, but she poured it away when no one was looking.

Now everyone set out, women with baskets, and men with knives, in order to cut up the buffalo. The woman remained alone in the village, but soon she got up and followed them, holding her belly and whimpering and crying.

'What is the matter with you, that you are following us?' asked her husband. 'If you are sick, stay at home!'

'No,' answered the woman, 'I did not want to be all alone.'

Her mother-in-law scolded her, saying that she could not understand what she was doing and that she would kill herself by this. When the men had finished cutting up the buffalo, and the women had filled the baskets with meat, she got up and said, 'Let me carry the head!'

'But no, you are sick, it is too heavy for you!'

'No,' she insisted, 'let me have it!' So she took it and carried it on her head.

When they arrived at the village, instead of going into the house, the woman went

129

into the hut where the cooking-pots were kept and put down the buffalo's head. Obstinately, she refused to move. Her husband came looking for her, to bring her into the house, saying she would be more comfortable there, but she only snapped at him, 'Do not disturb me!'

Then her mother-in-law came and admonished her gently. The woman replied crossly, 'Why do you all torment me? Will you not let me sleep even a little?'

Then they brought her some food, but she only pushed it away. Night came, and her husband went to bed. He did not sleep, however, but lay and listened.

The woman now fetched some fire, boiled some water in her little pot and stirred into it some of the medicine that she had brought with her. Then, taking the buffalo's head, she cut it with her little knife, close to the ear, where the bullet had gone in. Then she put her cupping horn over the wound and sucked, sucked with all her strength, until she succeeded in drawing first a few clots, and then liquid blood. Then she smeared the cuts with some of the fat in the gourd, and let the steam from the boiling medicinal water soften and soothe the wound. Then she sang this litany:

'Oh, my father, Rover of the Plain,

They told me, they told me, Oh Rover of the Plain:

They told me you would pass through deep darkness; that you would wander everywhere in the shadow, Oh Rover of the Plain;

You are the tender green plant growing among ruins, that dies too soon, consumed by a gnawing worm . . .

You who made flowers and fruits fall in your path, Oh Rover of the Plain!'

When she had finished her litany, the head moved, the limbs grew again, the buffalo came to life once more, shook his head and stretched . . .

But at that very moment the man, who could not sleep for worrying about his wife's strange behaviour, left the house, saying, 'Why does my wife have to cry so long? I must see what is the matter!' He came into the hut, and in a fury she cried, 'Leave me alone!' It was too late; the buffalo's head fell to the ground again mortally wounded, dead as before.

The man returned to the house, he had understood nothing

—'He came into the hut
. . . the buffalo's head fell
to the ground again . . .
dead as before.'

of all this and had seen nothing. Once again the woman took the pot, boiled the water and the medicinal roots, cut the wound and sucked blood with the cupping horn, anointed the wound and steamed it, and sang as before:

'Oh, my father, Rover of the Plain,

Indeed they told me truly that you would pass through deep darkness; that you would wander everywhere in the shadow, Oh Rover of the Plain;

You are the tender green plant growing among ruins, that dies too soon, consumed by a gnawing worm . . .

You who made flowers and fruits fall in your path, Oh Rover of the Plain!'

Once again, the buffalo got up, his limbs grew together again, he felt life in his body, shook his head – but then again came the man, full of anxiety, to see what his sick wife could be doing. She became very angry with him, but in spite of that he settled down in the hut to watch what she was doing. As she could not work her medicine in his company, she took her fire, her cooking pot and all the other things and went outside. She pulled up grass to make the fire burn hotter, and began to resuscitate the buffalo for the third time.

She was too late, the day was beginning and her mother-in-law came up – and once more the Rover's head fell to the ground, dead, and with the wound beginning to putrefy.

The woman then said to all of them, 'I want to go down to the lake alone, and bathe.'

These two carvings, which may represent female tribal ancestors, were collected in 1901 from the Anguru of Malawi.

Opposite: the Bavenda of Mozambique carve rhythmical guilloche patterns on their hut doors, and on the wooden keys of their xylophones.

They answered, 'But how will you get there? You are sick, and have not slept all night!'

She went off all the same and then came back and told them, 'On my way I met someone from my village. He told me that my mother is very, very ill. I asked him to come here to the village but he refused and said, "They would offer me food and that would delay me". He went on his way at once and said that I must hurry. So goodbye, I must go.'

Of course, this story was not true. She had thought of going to the lake so that she could tell this story and have a reason for visiting her people to bring them the news of the buffalo's death.

She went off, balancing her basket on her head and all the way she sang her litany of the Rover of the Plain. All along the road, the people banded together behind her to accompany her. When she arrived home, she told them that they had prophesied truly, and the buffalo was dead.

Then they sent out messengers in all directions to summon all the people of the tribe. They reproached the woman, saying, 'Do you see now? We did warn you. But you refused all the girls as servants and insisted on the buffalo. Now, in his death, you have killed us all!'

They were all lamenting like this when the man, who had followed his wife, arrived. He leaned his gun against a tree and sat down. They greeted him with bitter mockery, 'Hail, murderer, hail! You have killed us all!' He could not understand this, and wondered why they should call him murderer.

'I shot a buffalo, but what has that to do with it?' he said.

'Yes, but this buffalo was your wife's servant,' they replied. 'He drew water for her, cut wood, worked in the fields.'

The man was quite amazed and said, 'Why did no one tell me? I would not have killed him then.'

They replied, 'That is how it is. He is dead, and so we must all die as well.'

Thereupon all of the people began to cut their throats. First, the woman, who, as she did it, called out:

'Oh, my father, Rover of the Plain!'

Then came her parents, brothers, sisters, one after the other.

The Ndebele of Transvaal decorate the walls of their *lelapa*, or living enclosures, with a variety of geometric patterns.

A Zulu kraal, with its characteristic huts of thatched grass, seen among the rolling hills of Natal.

The first one said:
 'You would pass through deep darkness!'
The next:
 'You would wander everywhere in the shadow!'
The next:
 'You are the tender green plant that dies too soon!'
The next:
 'You made flowers and fruits fall in your path!'
All cut their throats and they even killed babies who were still in skins on their mother's backs. 'Why should we let them live,' they said, 'since they would only lose their minds!'
The man returned home and told his people how, by shooting the buffalo he had killed his wife and all her tribe. His parents said to him, 'Do you see now? Did we not warn you that you would find misfortune? We offered to find you a good wife from our own people, but you would have none of it, and wanted to choose for yourself. Now you have lost your bride-price. Who will give it back to you, since all your wife's people are dead, to whom you gave your wealth!'
This is the end.

135

Opposite: the Great Mosque at Kilwa was founded in the thirteenth century and extensively rebuilt in the fifteenth by Sultan Muhamad.

Right: a carving from the Bondei tribe of Tanzania representing a man in coastal Arab dress as worn by the Swahili.

Swahili peoples

The Swahili (Arab *sáhil,* coast) inhabit the islands of Pemba, Zanzibar, Mafia and the adjacent coast of East Africa between 2° and 9° S. They are a hybrid people of Arab stock mixed with Negro blood, some from coastal African tribes, some, through the slave trade, from further inland. In physical type they vary between Semitic Arab and full Negro, and their religion is predominantly Islam. Their language, Swahili, is the main *lingua franca* of East Africa, and is basically a Bantu-Arabic composite with added words from Persian and Indian, also English, Portuguese and German. Their literature is the most sophisticated to be found south of the Sahara. The towns of Kilwa and Pate have written histories from before A.D. 1500; the tales may be long and involved, showing considerable influence from the Middle East, while others are much more 'African.' The story chosen here is the latter half of one called *Sultan Majnun* which is really two distinct tales.

The history of the Swahili coast explains its hybrid culture. Persian and Arab traders ('Sindbad the Sailor') visited it from

The houses of the wealthier Arabs at Zanzibar would have had elaborately inlaid locks like these on their doors.

the earliest times and between the eighth and eleventh centuries many trading towns were founded, notably Mombasa, Kilwa, Kua, and Songo Mnara. These towns formed a merchant-city empire known as the Zinj empire, which resembled Venice in that its considerable wealth was based on an *entrepôt* sea trade on which very heavy imposts and tariff dues were levied. These do not seem to have deterred traders, especially those from India, who traded silks and export pottery from China, also glazed pottery, beads, carpets, silver, pearls and lengths of cotton in return for gold from Sofala, a few slaves, and above all, ivory, for which there was an insatiable demand. Probably as many as 1,500 elephants were killed each year; slaughter on this scale would indicate trade contacts between the Zinj empire and a large area of East and Central Africa. The Portuguese, arriving at the end of the fifteenth century, wrecked this highly organized Indian Ocean trade complex, thereby undermining the Zinj empire with its capital, Kilwa. The Portuguese were followed in the late sixteenth century by the Turks and by Zimba tribesmen from south of the Zambesi. The Imams of Muscat ruled this area from the seventeenth century onwards through local walis or viceroys. Zanzibar became the most important town in the nineteenth century and the Sultanate became a British Protectorate in 1890.

Nunda, eater of people
(Swahili, East Africa)

The Nunda, or *Mngwa* appears in many Swahili songs and tales, and appears to be a local equivalent to a dragon – a huge cat, distinct from a lion or a leopard, and as large as a donkey, with an aura of the supernatural that makes it invincible.

A long time ago there was a Sultan of Zanzibar called Majnùn and he was blessed with seven sons. The six elder sons filled him with joy and pride whenever he saw them, but the youngest one, who spent all his time among the womenfolk, filled him with shame and anger. The Sultan had talked to him, with no avail: he had beaten him, with no avail; he had tied him up, with no avail; and at last he grew tired of trying to make the youth change his ways, and left him alone.

Now this Sultan Majnùn had a date tree which was very beautiful. When the time came for this date tree to bear fruit for the first time, the Sultan looked forward eagerly to tasting

Throne, or official's chair, made of ebony inlaid with ivory, with twisted sinew 'caning', from Zanzibar.

Upper-class women in Zanzibar wore pattens like these in the
Turkish baths, and formerly wore them habitually.

it. But lo, on the morning when the dates were to be ripe for
eating, the tree was stripped bare. At this the Sultan was angry
and disappointed, and when the next crop of dates was about
to ripen, he set his eldest son to keep watch over the tree. The
young man was unable to keep awake, and in the morning
the tree was again stripped bare. When the next crop of dates
was about to ripen, the Sultan's second son volunteered to
guard the tree, but he also fell asleep, and again the tree was
stripped bare. It happened likewise with the third, fourth,
fifth and six sons. Every time a crop of dates was about to
ripen, they mounted guard and fell asleep, and awoke to find
all the dates gone. When the date tree bore dates for the eighth
time, the seventh son, who spent all his time among the
womenfolk, said that he would guard the tree. His brothers
mocked him for thinking that he would succeed where they
had failed, but the Sultan gave him leave to guard the tree,
reckoning that the dates were as good as lost in any case. The
youth kept awake by putting a thorn under his chin; a great
bird came to eat the dates, and he drove it away so that it
would never return, and in the morning he brought a dish of
dates to his father.

Sultan Majnùn also had a cat that was marked like a civet
cat, and this cat was very handsome, and growing fast. At

first this cat was content to eat the food provided for it, but as it grew larger, it grew hungrier and fiercer. And what this cat caught at the beginning was a hen's little chickens. They told the Sultan who said, 'The cat is mine and the chickens are mine, so that is all right.'

Two or three days passed and the cat caught a nanny-goat. And they told the Sultan, 'Master, the cat has caught a nanny-goat.' He replied, 'The goat was mine and the cat is mine.' And the people had to be content with that.

So they lived quietly, till a few days later, the Sultan's cat went away and caught a calf. The people came and told him, 'The cat has caught a calf.' And the Sultan answered, 'The cat is mine and the calf was mine.' They said, 'Very good, Master.'

Two days later, the cat caught a cow and the cow's owner went and complained to the Sultan, saying, 'Master, the cat has killed my cow.' But he only replied, 'It was my cow and my cat.'

And the cat killed nothing for a few days, and then it caught

This splendid leopard, one of a pair from Benin, Nigeria, is composed of five large elephant tusks inlaid with bronze spots.

a donkey. So they told the Sultan, 'Master, the cat has caught a donkey,' to which he said, 'My cat and my donkey.' The very next day it killed a horse, and when they told the Sultan of this, he replied, 'My cat and my horse.' The cat waited a while and then it caught a camel. The people told the Sultan, who got angry and said, 'What are you talking about? It is my camel and my cat; you do not like this cat and want me to kill it, every time telling me mere tales. And I will not kill it; let it eat the camel, let it eat even a man.'

The cat waited until the next day, and then it caught a child. And the child's parents came lamenting, saying, 'Master, the cat has taken our child.' The Sultan said, 'The cat is mine and the child is mine.' Then the next day the cat caught a woman, and when he was told of this the Sultan said, 'The cat is mine and the woman is mine.'

After this the cat left the town and went to live in the thickets alongside the Mnazimoja road that led to the mainland. If anyone passed along that road, going for sweet water to drink, the cat sprang out and devoured him. If the cat saw a cow or a goat on the way to pasture, it seized it and ate it. Every living thing that it saw passing on that road became its prey.

The people went in a body to the Sultan, and appealed to him, saying, 'Hear us, Master. It is you who are our Sultan, it is you who are our Master, it is you who are our shield. Master, you have left that cat to its own devices too long. It has gone to live on the Mnazimoja road, and if a man passes, it eats him; if a cow passes, it eats it; if a donkey passes, it eats it; if a goat passes, it eats it. Whatever living thing goes on the Mnazimoja road is caught and eaten, and at night the cat comes down into the town, to catch and eat whatever it can find there. So then, Master, what are we to do, with things in this state?'

The Sultan replied angrily, 'I think you hate this cat in your souls; you want me to have it killed and I refuse to; the cat is mine, and all these things it eats are mine.'

The people were dismayed; there was no one who dared to

—'The Sultan went first followed by his six sons . . . The cat sprang out of the thicket and killed three of the sons.'

342

kill the cat, which was now an invincible and insatiable monster. And then, as people gave up using the Mnazimoja road, by which it lived, it moved to live alongside another road, killing and eating in the same way.

Again the people went and told the Sultan, 'The cat is terrorizing us all.' And the Sultan replied in anger, 'I hate your messages, they are worthless. I will not listen to such gossip, neither will I kill the cat.'

The people stopped using the second road that the cat used as its base, and so it moved to another road and did as before. And they told the Sultan, 'The cat has got worse, Master, it has become exceedingly dangerous and seizes everything.' He replied, 'The cat is mine and all that it takes are mine.' So the people stopped going along that road also.

The messages and complaints about the cat became so tiresome and frequent that the Sultan placed a man at the door of his audience-room, telling him 'Anyone who comes here with complaints against the cat must be sent away.' The man said 'All right, Master.'

Well then, at night the cat used to come into the town, seizing everything it could get hold of, and in the morning it would leave for the country. At last there were no people living in houses outside the town walls. Those who ran away had already run away, and those who were caught had been caught. And now the cat moved a little further out into the country, catching people and animals as it went, and every night it would come and raid the town for whatever it could seize and eat. And no one was able to approach the Sultan to tell him what the cat was doing.

Till one day the Sultan said to his sons, 'Today I am going to look at my country and my people, let us all go.' So the Sultan set out, accompanied by his six elder sons. They left the palace and went on until they passed a thicket by the roadside; the Sultan went first, followed by his six sons. The cat sprang out of the thicket and killed three of the sons. All the people who were there cried out, 'The cat! The cat!! The

The richer Arab houses at Zanzibar and elsewhere had elaborately carved doors and door-frames with Indian-inspired patterns.

Swahili women are very skilful in making prayer mats like these, with Arabic inscriptions plaited into the design.

cat!!!' And the Sultan's bodyguard said, 'Master, let us look for it, and kill it.' And the Sultan urged them on to do so, and they replied, 'All right, Master.'

Now the Sultan said, 'This creature is no longer a cat, it is Nunda, a demon which came and snatched away from me even my sons.' And the people, relieved that the Sultan was aware at last of the cat's misdeeds, came to him and said, 'Master, the cat is no respecter of persons, saying, "This is the Master's son, let me leave him alone; or, this is the Master's wife, let me leave her alone; or this is the Master's kinsman, let me leave him." The cat has nothing in it to make it selective, it devours everything; we fear, Master, that it may even eat you.' And the Sultan agreed with this. The people went on to say, 'Did we not tell you, Master, how the cat was eating people, and you said, "My cat and my people."' And the Sultan admitted this also.

And of the soldiers that went to kill the cat some were killed and some ran away. The Sultan returned with his sons, and buried the three that were killed.

The seventh son, he that spent all his time with the womenfolk, had been in the palace while this was happening. When he heard the news of his three brothers, that had been killed by the cat, he resolved to find the Nunda. He went to his mother and told her, 'I too will go, so that the cat may kill me as it has killed my brothers.' His mother was surprised, and asked, 'How will you go, son? By yourself?' And he answered, 'I shall go in anger; shall not a man feel anger, to lose three brothers in one day? Therefore I shall wander about and look for this cat, this Nunda which killed my brothers.' To this his mother answered, 'Very well my son, but I do not want you to go. Three have died, and if you die also, is not that one grief more?' Yet the prince insisted, 'I must go, mother and do not tell my father.'

Accordingly his mother prepared food for the youth, both rice and cakes, and gave him two trusted slaves, Shindano and Kiroboto, to carry the food and other baggage. She also gave him a great spear, and his sword, and all three of them took their guns. Thus equipped he went out after the cat, which had run off to a great distance.

Soon after the prince left the town, he tracked down a civet

They are made of shredded and dyed palm leaves, plaited into long strips about 1½ inches wide, then sewn together.

147

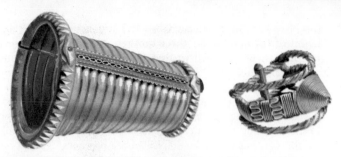

The silversmiths of the Swahili coast produce armlets and anklets that owe more to Arab than to African culture.

cat, and he killed it, and bound it, and dragged it, and as he came into the town he sang

'Oh mother, I have killed
The Nunda, eater of people.'

But his mother answered him, singing

'My son, this is not he,
The Nunda, eater of people.'

And she said 'My son, this is not it, the Nunda is larger, leave it now my son, and stay at home.' But her pleas were of no avail; the youth answered, 'Mother, I cannot help going to avenge my brothers.'

The prince went deeper into the forest, and saw a larger kind of civet cat, and he tracked it down and killed it and bound it. And when he was halfway back to the town he sang

'Oh mother, I have killed
The Nunda, eater of people.'

And she answered him, singing

'My son, this is not he,
The Nunda, eater of people.'

So he threw it away. Then his mother said, 'Where do you think you will find this Nunda? It is far off, you do not know where; I beg you to stay at home.' And the youth replied, 'Mother, I shall obtain one of three things from God. And the first is, that I shall die; the second is that I shall find the Nunda and kill it; and the third is that I shall fail to find the Nunda and come back.' His mother answered, 'For myself, my son, I should like you to find this Nunda, and kill it, and return with it so that I may see it and have peace of mind.'

So the prince went out into the country again, and found a zebra, and he followed it and killed it and bound it and brought it back to the town. And when he came near the town gates he sang

'Oh mother, I have killed

The Nunda, eater of people.'

And his mother answered him, singing,

'My son, this is not he,

The Nunda, eater of people.'

So he threw it away, and went out into the wilderness again and he killed a giraffe and brought it back; he killed a rhinoceros, and brought it back; he killed even an elephant and brought it back; every time he returned with some large wild beast, singing

'Oh mother, I have killed

The Nunda, eater of people.'

Brass figure of a royal hunter armed with a dane gun and accompanied by his dog, from the Fon, Dahomey.

And every time his mother answered him, singing

'My son, this is not he,

The Nunda, eater of people.'

The prince went on searching, a long way off, for many days, and he killed numerous wild animals but still he could not track down the Nunda. There was no beast, however large or fierce, that he was afraid of, and at last his mother and father, both weeping, begged him to abandon the hunt, saying, 'We are afraid our youngest son will die, the best son that we have. But what shall we do? He will not stay at home.'

The prince went out searching again in the forest and wilderness but still he could not find the Nunda. The Sultan, his father, offered him the crown itself, and begged him to stay, and be Sultan, if only he would leave his quest, and not go out into the forest. But the youth went away again hunting the Nunda.

Many times he and his slaves thought they had found the Nunda, and many times were mistaken. And he went further into the wilderness, and one day he passed a great forest and saw a great hill and a path going along towards the bottom of the hill. And he and his slaves ate and drank and slept. The next morning they awoke, and the slaves asked the young prince for his instructions. And first he told them to rub the sticks to make fire, and cook some rice, that they might eat quickly, for the youth's soul told him that on this day he would find the Nunda at last. So they all ate the rice, and then they started to climb the great hill. And they went on till they reached the top and could see a long way all round. So the youth said, 'Let us rest here on the top, and sleep here till tomorrow, and make our plans.' The slaves said, 'Very well, Master.'

And one of the slaves, called Shindano, got up and walked around the top of the great hill. When he looked down, there was a great beast, but he could not see it clearly through the trees. So he called, 'Master! Master!!' And the young prince went to where the slave stood and looked down, and his soul told him that this was the Nunda at last.

—'And they came yet closer to it .. The Nunda did not move, these guns had done their work.'

151

He went down with his gun in his hand, and his spear, till he got half way down the hillside, and could look closer. He said to himself, 'This must be the Nunda. My mother told me its ears were small, and this one's are small. She told me it was broad and not long, and this is broad and not long; she told me it was marked like a civet cat, and this is marked like a civet cat; she told me its tail was thick, and this one's tail is thick; all these characteristics which my mother told me of are there.'

And he went back to his slaves and said, 'Let us eat well today.' So they ate a good meal and then they were ready. The youth told them to leave some food and water to one side for them to eat later on. It was now afternoon so they started off. And when they were half way down the slaves became frightened. So the young prince said to them, 'Come on, do not be afraid; there are two things in the world, living and dying. What then are you frightened about?' They answered, 'Very good, let us go on, Master.' They reached the bottom of the hill, and there was a forest. And the youth said, 'Each one

—'And all the people answered, singing many times, "My son, this one is he, the Nunda, eater of people."'

of us that wears two cloths should take one off, in case we get caught by the thorns, or we get chased and have to run for it. It is better for us to wear one cloth each, and tuck it up between our legs.' They did this, and then crept along till they saw the Nunda where it lay sleeping in the shade. And they came yet closer to it and saw it clearly. When the prince fired his gun his slaves fired also. The Nunda did not move, these guns had done their work. And they ran away and climbed up the mountain.

The sun was setting when they reached the top, and they took out their food and ate freely, and drank water, and then slept till morning, when they had breakfast. And then they went round to the back of the great hill and found that the Nunda was indeed dead. The youth rejoiced, and his slaves rejoiced.

And the youth said, 'Let us tie it up and take it along.' So they brought it home, and when they were near they began singing

'Oh Mother, I have killed

Arab traders in their dhows sailed between the Swahili coast of East Africa, Muscat, Arabia, Persia and even India.

The Nunda, eater of people.'
And they came nearer to the town, and went on singing
'Mother, mother, mother,
I come, from the evil spirits, to sing.
Mother, mother, mother,
I come from the evil spirits to sing,
From the evil spirits to sing,
Oh Mother, I have killed
The Nunda, eater of people.'
And his mother, and all the people, answered, singing many times
'My son, this one is he,
The Nunda, eater of people.'
When the Sultan heard that his son had returned, and had killed the Nunda, he felt there was no son as great as this one. And all the people in the town, free and slave, came to him, bringing presents. And he was beloved by all. When the third day came, the Sultan stepped down from his throne, and gave

154

it to his son, asking only for food and clothing for himself.

He gave orders about the Nunda, and its body was carried, and put in a pit, and the pit was dug deep, and filled in well. And he built a house over the pit of the Nunda, and stationed a soldier there, telling him, 'Every one that passes by on this road must give the usual present as thank-offering, and if he gives nothing, kill him.'

The prince lived with his parents a long time and he took a wife, and lived in happiness. And then his father and his mother were taken by necessity, and died, and he mourned for them. And when the time for mourning was over, the youth remained as Sultan, for his father had given him the dignity before his death, and of his three brothers, the eldest became vizier, the middle one chief officer, and the last became his secretary. And they all lived in harmony.

This is the story that Chuma made about Sultan Majnùn, and this is the end of the story. If it is good, the goodness belongs to us all, and if it is bad, the badness belongs to me alone who made it.

—'This is the end of the story. . . . If it is bad, the badness belongs to me alone who made it.'

SUDAN

44.

3. GUINEA
SIERRA
LEONE
14. GHANA
IVORY 2.
COAST

36. 23. 26.
38. NIGERIA

DAHOMEY 25.
48. 17. 24.
22.

CENTRAL AFRICAN
CAMEROUN REPUBLIC
47.

37.
21.
41.
9.

UGANDA
4. KENYA
27. 28.
40. 1.
45. 39. 46. 29.
8. 30.
TANZANIA 49.
42.
32.

6.
CONGO
16. 12.
5.

11.
33. ZAMBIA
7.

MALAWI
31.
32a MOZAMBIQUE

RHODESIA
34. 50.
SOUTH-WEST
AFRICA BOTSWANA 15.
10.
43.
18. 35.
13.

FURTHER READING

P. Radin & J. J. Sweeney, *African Folktales and Sculpture,* 1953
C. G. Seligman, *Races of Africa,* 1957
G. Parrinder, *African Mythology,* 1967

The stories in this book have come from the following sources:-
W. H. I. Bleek, *Reynard the Fox in South Africa,* 1864. E. Dayrell, *Folk Stories from Southern Nigeria,* 1910. J. Gabus, *Au Sahara, Vol. I, Les Hommes et leurs Outils,* 1954. R. Huffman, *Nuer Customs and Folklore,* 1931. P. Itayemi & P. Gurrey, *Folktales and Fables,* 1953. H. A. S. Johnston, *A Selection of Hausa Stories,* 1966. H. A. Junod, *Les Baronga,* 1898. J. S. Mbiti, *Akamba Stories,* 1966. R. S. Rattray, *Akan-Ashanti Folk-Tales,* 1930. J. Roscoe, *The Baganda, Their Customs and Beliefs,* 1911. W. S. & K. Routledge, *With a Prehistoric People: the Akikuyu of British East Africa,* 1910. E. W. Smith & A. M. Dale, *The Ila-Speaking Peoples of Northern Rhodesia,* 1920. E. Steere, *Swahili Tales,* 1870. E. Torday, *On the Trail of the Bushongo,* 1925.

Museums

The objects illustrated belong to the public and private collections listed below, which include most of the principal ethnographical museums in Western Europe, where many more African sculptures and exhibits may be seen. The name of the museum or collection is followed by the page reference of the illustration concerned.

British Museum, London:- 6, 8r, 13 lower *l*, 14, 15*l*, 18, 19, 22, 25, 29, 38, 39, 42, 43, 45, 51, 53, 55, 62, 63, 67 (head only), 74r, 75, 80, 90, 91, 94, 99, 107r, 112, 113, 115, 116, 124, 127, 129, 140, 141, 148; Horniman Museum, London:- 137; Wallace Collection, London:- 26; Roland Penrose:- 105; Manchester University Museum, Manchester:- 99; Pitt-Rivers Museum, Oxford:- 52; Musée de l'Homme, Paris:- 40, 84, 89, 110, 127; Charles Ratton:- 16; Pierre Vérité:- 56; Musée Royal de l'Afrique Centrale, Tervuren:- 104, 106, 111; Musée d'Ethnographie, Antwerp:- 125; Museum für Volkerkunde, Berlin:- 17, 46, 74*l*, 83, 85, 103, 120, 133; Linden-Museum, Stuttgart:- 82, 86, 87, 102, 119, 121; Sammlung für Volkerkunde der Universitat Zürich:- 8*l*, 67 (body and horse), 109; Eliot Elisofon:- 107*l*, 114; Museum Rietburg, Zürich:- 15r, 109; Náprstek Museum, Prague:- 98; Museum of Ethnography, Leningrad:- 35; Nigerian Museum, Lagos:- 41, 45, 47; Ife Museum, Nigeria:- 13r; Jos Museum, Nigeria:- 13 upper *l*; University Museum, Philadelphia:- 28; Margaret Webster Plass:- 21, 23, 149;

INDEX

Page numbers in bold type refer
to illustrations

SOME OTHER TITLES IN THIS SERIES